The CBT
Art Workbook for
Coping with Depression

Part of the CBT Art Workbooks for Mental and Emotional Wellbeing series

The CBT Art Workbooks for Mental and Emotional Wellbeing series provides creative CBT information and worksheets for adults to manage and understand a variety of emotional issues. Suitable for adults in individual or group therapeutic work, they are an excellent resource to use in conjunction with professional therapy or for adults to use themselves to improve and maintain mental wellbeing.

Also part of the CBT Art Workbooks for Mental and Emotional Wellbeing series

The CBT Art Workbook for Coping with Anxiety
Jennifer Guest
ISBN 978 1 78775 012 8
eISBN 978 1 78775 013 5

By the same author

The Art Activity Book for Psychotherapeutic Work
100 Illustrated CBT and Psychodynamic Handouts for Creative Therapeutic Work
Jennifer Guest
ISBN 978 1 78592 301 2
eISBN 978 1 78450 607 0

The Art Activity Book for Relational Work
100 illustrated therapeutic worksheets to use with individuals, couples and families
Jennifer Guest
ISBN 978 1 78592 160 5
eISBN 978 1 78450 428 1

The CBT Art Activity Book
100 illustrated handouts for creative therapeutic work
Jennifer Guest
ISBN 978 1 84905 665 6
eISBN 978 1 78450 168 6

The CBT
Art Workbook for
Coping with Depression

Part of the CBT Art Workbooks for
Mental and Emotional Wellbeing *series*

Jennifer Guest

Jessica Kingsley Publishers
London and Philadelphia

First published in 2020
by Jessica Kingsley Publishers
73 Collier Street
London N1 9BE, UK
and
400 Market Street, Suite 400
Philadelphia, PA 19106, USA

www.jkp.com

Library of Congress Cataloging in Publication Data
A CIP catalog record for this book is available from the Library of Congress

British Library Cataloguing in Publication Data
A CIP catalogue record for this book is available from the British Library

ISBN 978 1 78775 096 8
eISBN 978 1 78775 097 5

Printed and bound in the United States

Acknowledgements

I would like to express many thanks to all my clients and colleagues, who, over the years have helped bring this workbook into being. Grateful appreciation goes to the theorists who have devoted their lives and careers to helping people experience happier, healthier and more peaceful lives. I've given credit to theorists where I've knowingly designed a worksheet from their work, and there are some pages designed from techniques I've come across over the years which I'm unfortunately unable to give specific credit to. No worksheets have been created without acknowledging the source where this is known. Thanks also to everyone involved at Jessica Kingsley Publishers for their support and input.

Contents

About This book

This workbook offers an opportunity for those experiencing mild to moderate depression to help manage and cope with the symptoms using tools from cognitive behavioural therapy (CBT) approaches. I've worked with many clients experiencing depression over the years and have found CBT ideas have been incredibly successful in helping to reduce symptoms, as well as for learning ways to help manage them. It's a privilege to be able to share these ideas with you here, and I sincerely hope this workbook has a positive impact on your life and your wellbeing. This book can be used autonomously or in conjunction with therapy. It's not intended to be used as a replacement for CBT, if therapeutic input would be beneficial. Please ensure that access to professional support is available if you experience any unexpected or overwhelming emotional reactions as a result of working through this book, or your symptoms become more severe. You might choose to focus on the pages most relevant to you, or work through the entire book from beginning to end.

Introduction

INTRODUCTION

This workbook follows steps used in cognitive behavioural therapy (CBT).

These aim to:

- Explore the nature of the problem
- Gather information by monitoring depression levels
- Recognise the links between thoughts, emotions, physiological responses and behaviour
- Explore unhelpful thinking patterns, beliefs and behaviours
- Teach how to implement more positive and realistic thinking and reactions

These steps help us to develop healthy behaviours and thought patterns, to increase our emotional wellbeing and mental health, thereby reducing levels of depression.

EVIDENCE

The influential 'Depression Report', by Lord Layard (2006) states how he has 'taken a very positive view of the role of CBT, as a means of addressing and reducing the current high levels of depression…within society.'

Jenkins 2017, p.20

NICE GUIDELINES

The National Institute for Health and Care Excellence (NICE) recommendations for the use of psychological therapies for mild depression in adults include self-help approaches and brief CBT.

Jenkins 2017

WHY ART?

Having worked within the therapeutic world for nearly two decades, I consider delivering therapy as one of my passions, alongside art.

Making art has been personally therapeutic during times when I've experienced emotional challenges and high levels of stress in my life.

I've witnessed the benefits of art-making and using visual ways of expression and processing with many clients. At the very least this is a way to encourage relaxation, and, on a more profound level, it can facilitate deeper change. The ideas in this workbook provide a focus for coping with and reducing symptoms of mild to moderate depression through the use of creativity.

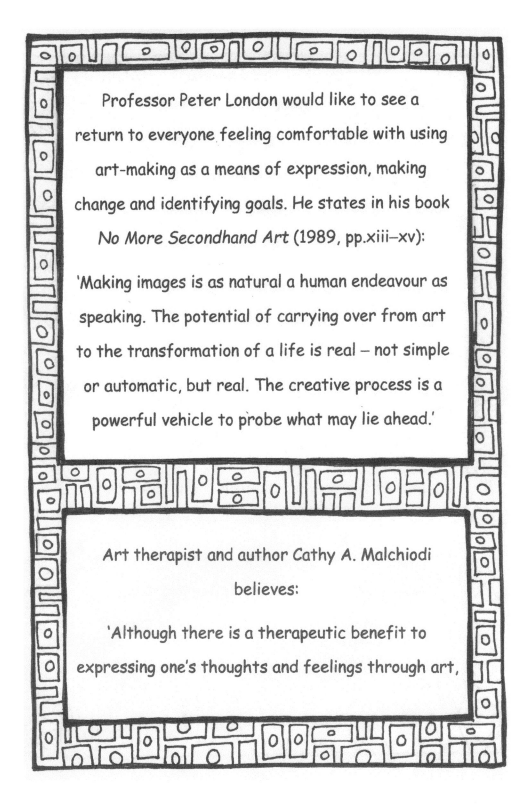

Professor Peter London would like to see a return to everyone feeling comfortable with using art-making as a means of expression, making change and identifying goals. He states in his book *No More Secondhand Art* (1989, pp.xiii–xv):

'Making images is as natural a human endeavour as speaking. The potential of carrying over from art to the transformation of a life is real – not simple or automatic, but real. The creative process is a powerful vehicle to probe what may lie ahead.'

Art therapist and author Cathy A. Malchiodi believes:

'Although there is a therapeutic benefit to expressing one's thoughts and feelings through art, one of the most impressive aspects of the art process is its potential to achieve or restore psychological equilibrium. Art can be used...to repair, restore and heal.' (2007, p.134)

'Engaging in activities such as painting and sculpting, along with having a positive outlook, boosts the immune system and may even eliminate depressive and sleep disorders.' (2007, p.175)

GO BIG

If you prefer to produce artwork on a larger scale, please don't feel restricted by the page sizes here. You could transfer the ideas onto bigger pieces of paper or canvasses, or make 3D sculptures of your images.

1

What Is Depression?

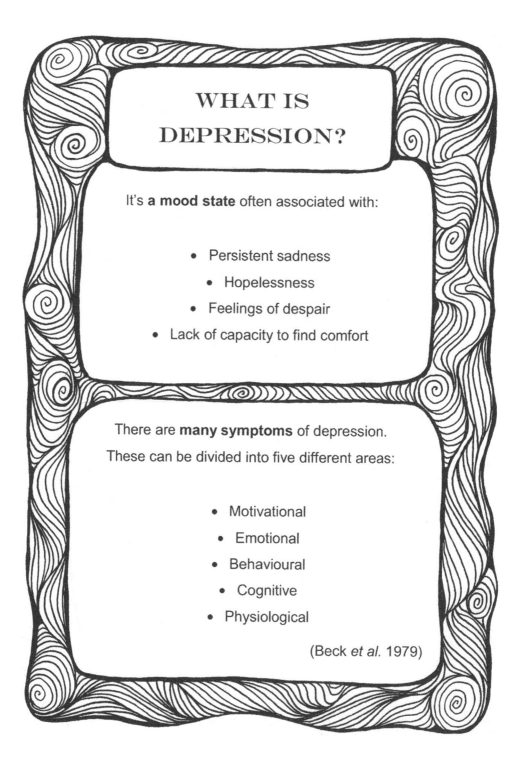

WHAT IS DEPRESSION?

It's **a mood state** often associated with:

- Persistent sadness
- Hopelessness
- Feelings of despair
- Lack of capacity to find comfort

There are **many symptoms** of depression.

These can be divided into five different areas:

- Motivational
- Emotional
- Behavioural
- Cognitive
- Physiological

(Beck *et al.* 1979)

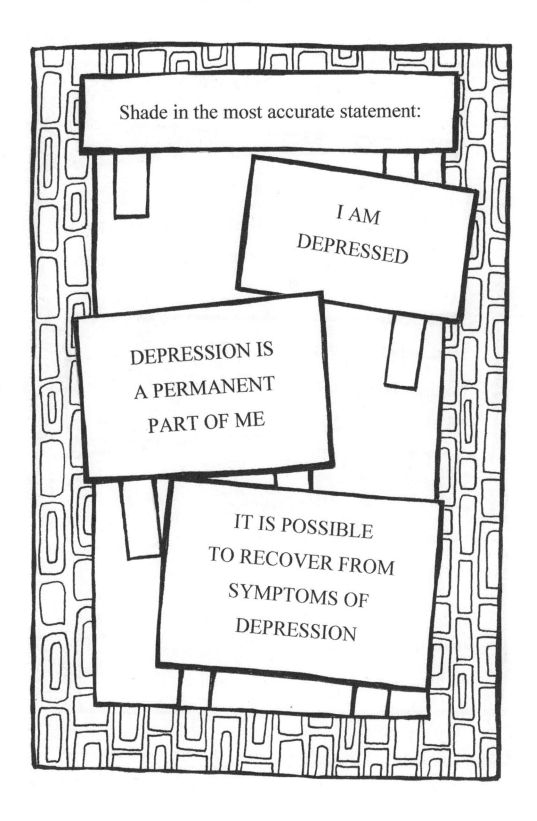

Shade in the most accurate statement:

I AM DEPRESSED

DEPRESSION IS A PERMANENT PART OF ME

IT IS POSSIBLE TO RECOVER FROM SYMPTOMS OF DEPRESSION

Different types of depression

Dysthymia

This is a mild depression which lasts for at least two years, and is sometimes described as chronic depression.

Seasonal Affective Disorder (SAD)

This usually impacts during the wintertime, although not always.

Prenatal depression

This happens during pregnancy.

Postnatal depression

This can become apparent following the birth of a child, and although it is usually diagnosed in mothers, it can affect fathers as well.

(Dunn 2016)

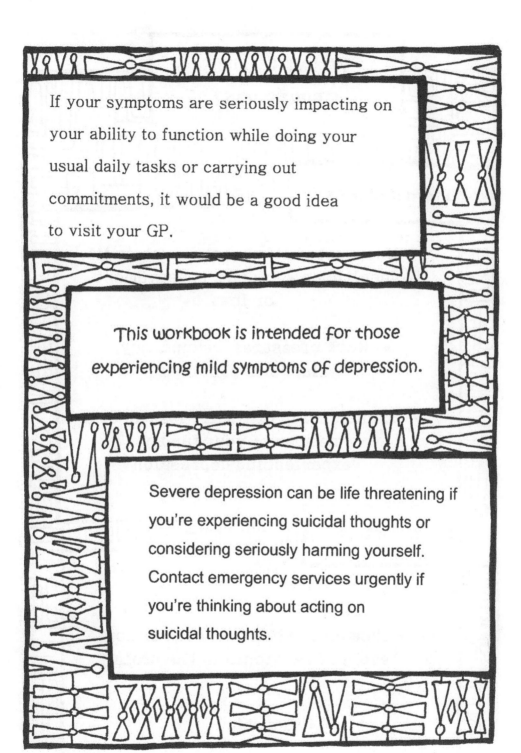

If your symptoms are seriously impacting on your ability to function while doing your usual daily tasks or carrying out commitments, it would be a good idea to visit your GP.

This workbook is intended for those experiencing mild symptoms of depression.

Severe depression can be life threatening if you're experiencing suicidal thoughts or considering seriously harming yourself. Contact emergency services urgently if you're thinking about acting on suicidal thoughts.

WHAT CAUSES DEPRESSION?

External factors

- Unexpected life events, such as ill health, an accident, bereavement or loss

- Work pressures, redundancy, financial problems

- Relationship or family issues, or a member of your family experiencing depression

Internal factors

- A chemical imbalance, such as low levels of serotonin in the brain

- Genetics

'Research shows that going through lots of smaller challenging experiences can have a bigger impact on your vulnerability to depression than experiencing one major traumatic event.

Difficult experiences during your childhood can have a big impact on your self-esteem and how you learned to cope with difficult emotions and situations. This can make you feel less able to cope with life's ups and downs, and lead to depression later in life.'

(Dunn 2016, p.10)

GRIEF

This is a natural process as a response to losing someone from our life. It can often result in feeling low for a short or long period of time. Pressure to *get over* a loss within a certain time frame can often add to symptoms of depression.

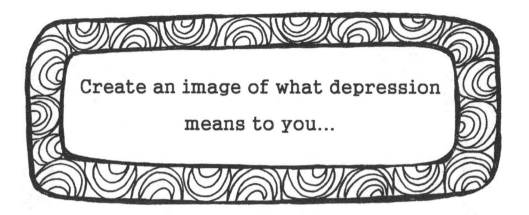

Create an image of what depression means to you...

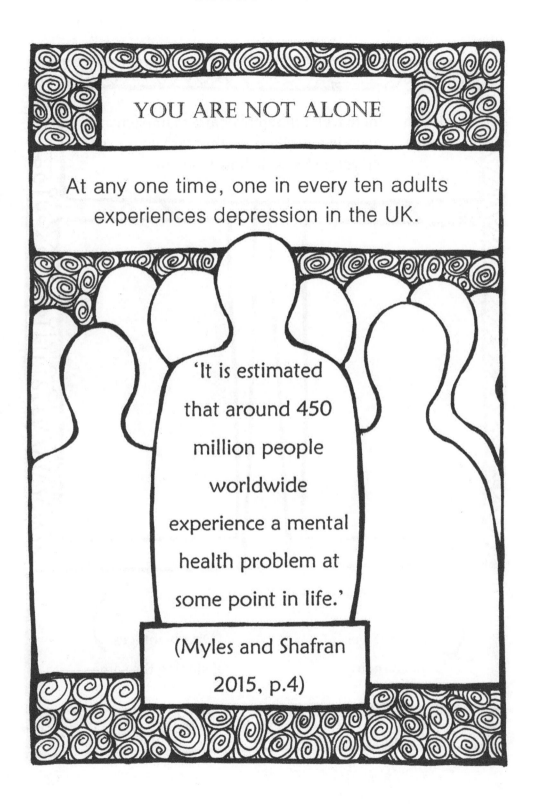

YOU ARE NOT ALONE

At any one time, one in every ten adults experiences depression in the UK.

'It is estimated that around 450 million people worldwide experience a mental health problem at some point in life.'

(Myles and Shafran 2015, p.4)

If you want to feel differently or aim to implement some changes in your lifestyle, this workbook can help you to focus on how to do this.

Draw or describe some...

Advantages
of changing

Disadvantages
of staying the same

2

What Is CBT?

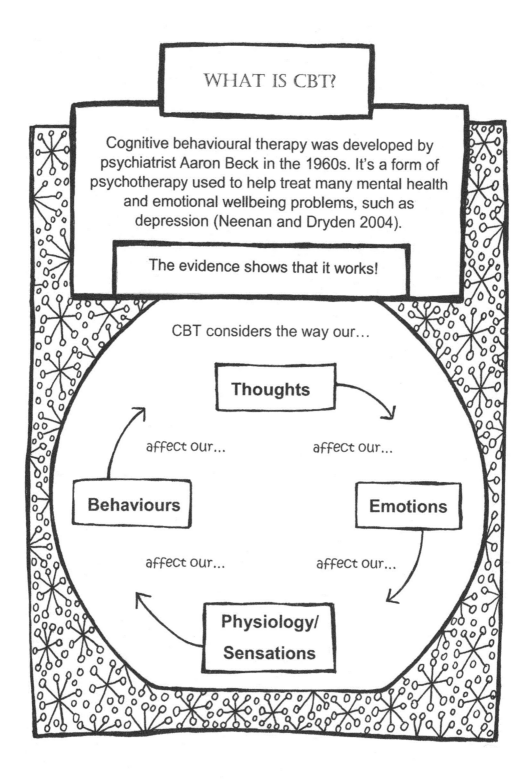

WHAT IS CBT?

Cognitive behavioural therapy was developed by psychiatrist Aaron Beck in the 1960s. It's a form of psychotherapy used to help treat many mental health and emotional wellbeing problems, such as depression (Neenan and Dryden 2004).

The evidence shows that it works!

CBT considers the way our…

Thoughts

affect our…

affect our…

Behaviours

Emotions

affect our…

affect our…

Physiology/ Sensations

'The aim of CBT techniques is to disrupt negative thought patterns, so they no longer arouse unbearable emotions.

Recognising thoughts as "just thoughts", rather than mistaking them for true perceptions or impulses that must be acted on, produces a calmer, more positive state of mind.'

(Barford 2018, p.35)

Depression can be intensified by thinking negatively about our:

- Selves
- Achievements
- Ability to cope
- Capacity to access help/support
- Future accomplishments
- Health

Colour in the ticks if any of these are the focus of negative thinking for you.

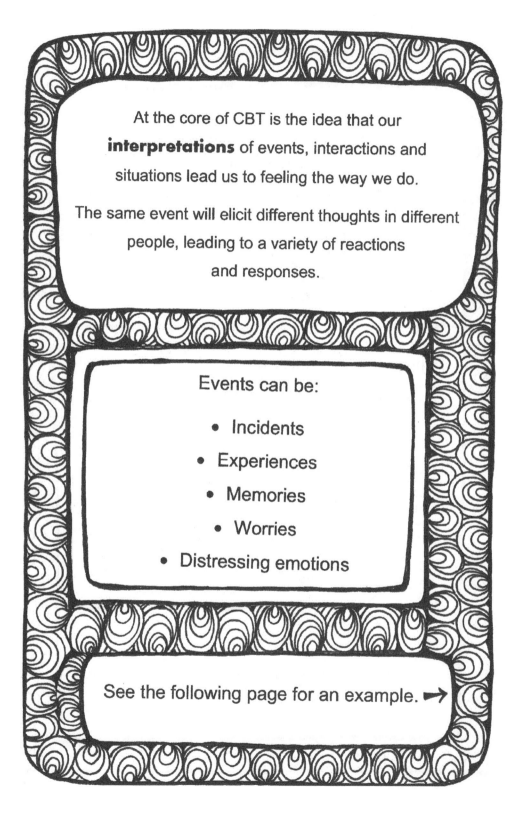

At the core of CBT is the idea that our **interpretations** of events, interactions and situations lead us to feeling the way we do.

The same event will elicit different thoughts in different people, leading to a variety of reactions and responses.

Events can be:

- Incidents
- Experiences
- Memories
- Worries
- Distressing emotions

See the following page for an example. ➡

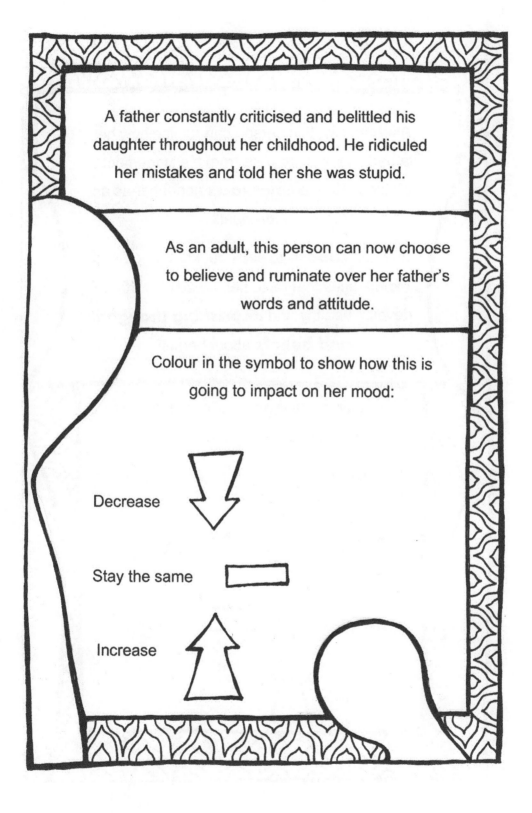

A father constantly criticised and belittled his daughter throughout her childhood. He ridiculed her mistakes and told her she was stupid.

As an adult, this person can now choose to believe and ruminate over her father's words and attitude.

Colour in the symbol to show how this is going to impact on her mood:

Decrease

Stay the same

Increase

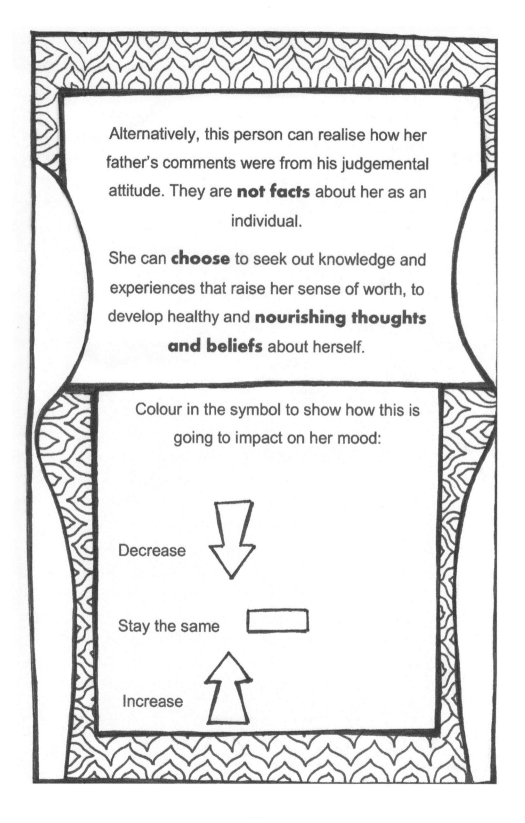

Alternatively, this person can realise how her father's comments were from his judgemental attitude. They are **not facts** about her as an individual.

She can **choose** to seek out knowledge and experiences that raise her sense of worth, to develop healthy and **nourishing thoughts and beliefs** about herself.

Colour in the symbol to show how this is going to impact on her mood:

Decrease

Stay the same

Increase

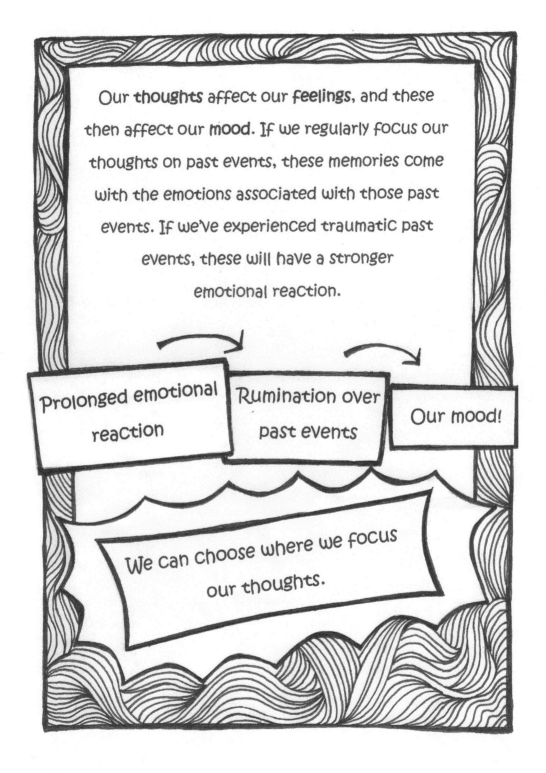

Our **thoughts** affect our **feelings**, and these then affect our **mood**. If we regularly focus our thoughts on past events, these memories come with the emotions associated with those past events. If we've experienced traumatic past events, these will have a stronger emotional reaction.

Prolonged emotional reaction

Rumination over past events

Our mood!

We can choose where we focus our thoughts.

3

Observations

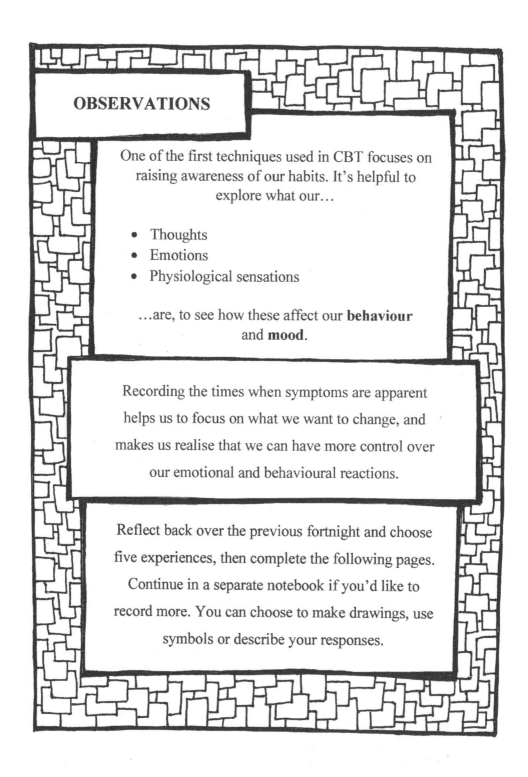

OBSERVATIONS

One of the first techniques used in CBT focuses on raising awareness of our habits. It's helpful to explore what our…

- Thoughts
- Emotions
- Physiological sensations

…are, to see how these affect our **behaviour** and **mood**.

Recording the times when symptoms are apparent helps us to focus on what we want to change, and makes us realise that we can have more control over our emotional and behavioural reactions.

Reflect back over the previous fortnight and choose five experiences, then complete the following pages. Continue in a separate notebook if you'd like to record more. You can choose to make drawings, use symbols or describe your responses.

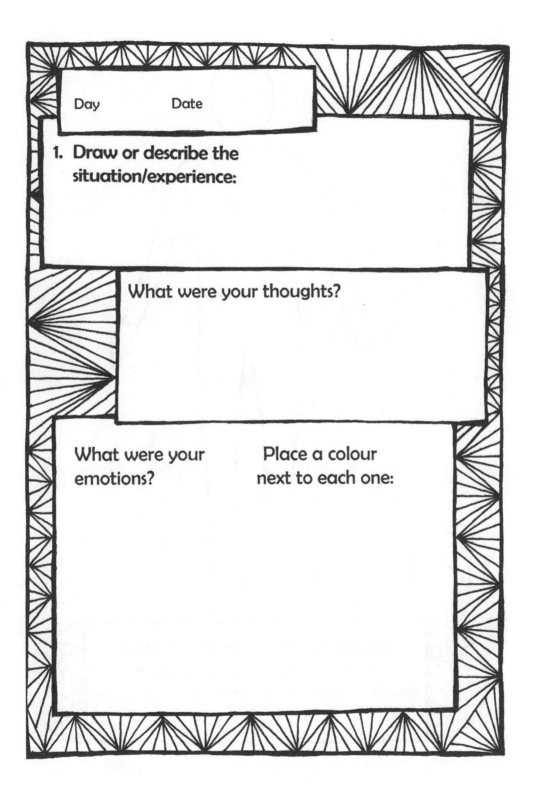

Day   Date

1. **Draw or describe the situation/experience:**

What were your thoughts?

What were your emotions?   **Place a colour next to each one:**

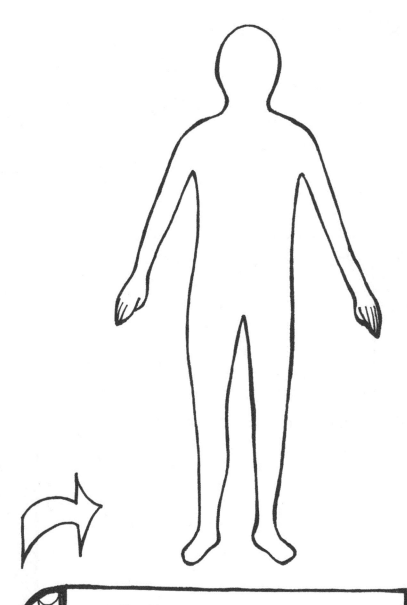

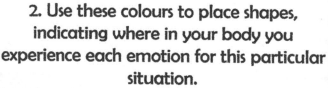

2. Use these colours to place shapes, indicating where in your body you experience each emotion for this particular situation.

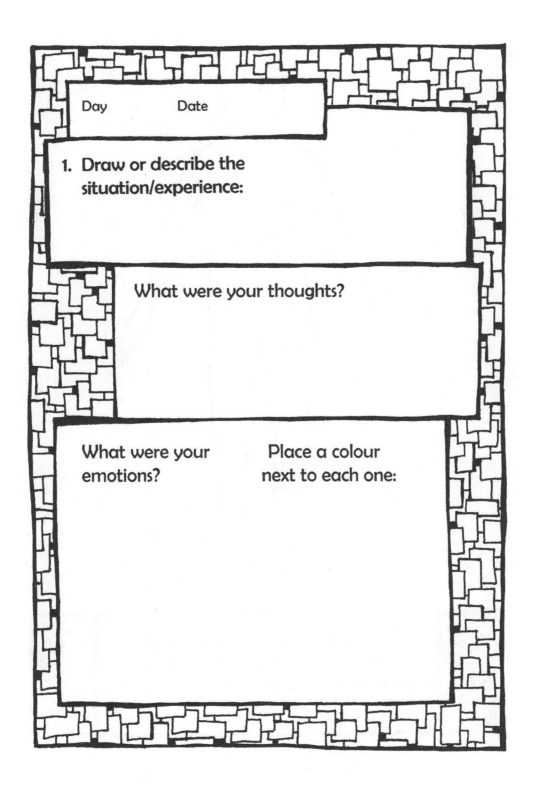

Day   Date

1. Draw or describe the situation/experience:

What were your thoughts?

What were your emotions?   Place a colour next to each one:

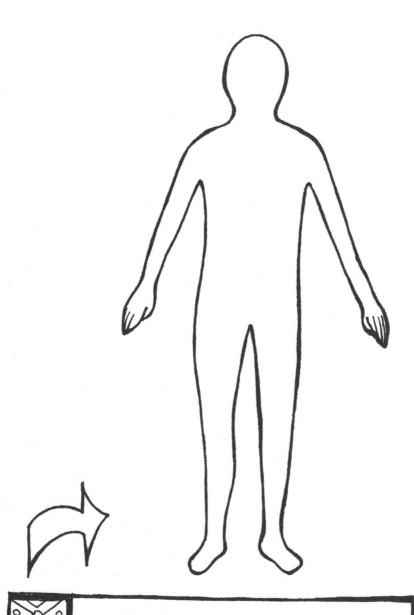

2. Use these colours to place shapes, indicating where in your body you experience each emotion for this particular situation.

Day   Date

1. Draw or describe the
   situation/experience:

What were your thoughts?

What were your   Place a colour
emotions?   next to each one:

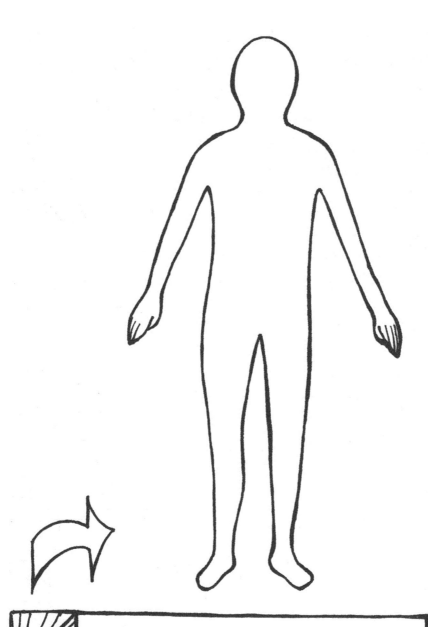

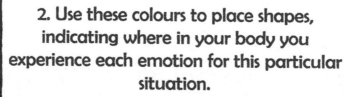

2. Use these colours to place shapes, indicating where in your body you experience each emotion for this particular situation.

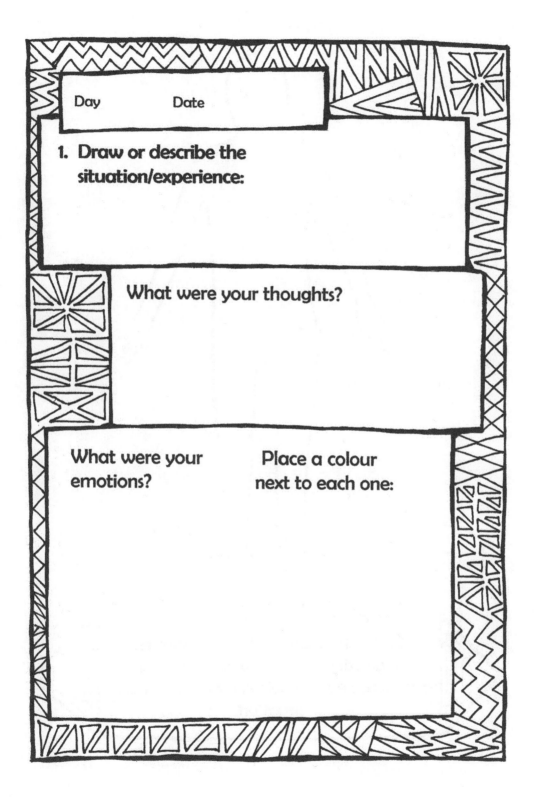

Day   Date

1. Draw or describe the
   situation/experience:

What were your thoughts?

What were your   Place a colour
emotions?   next to each one:

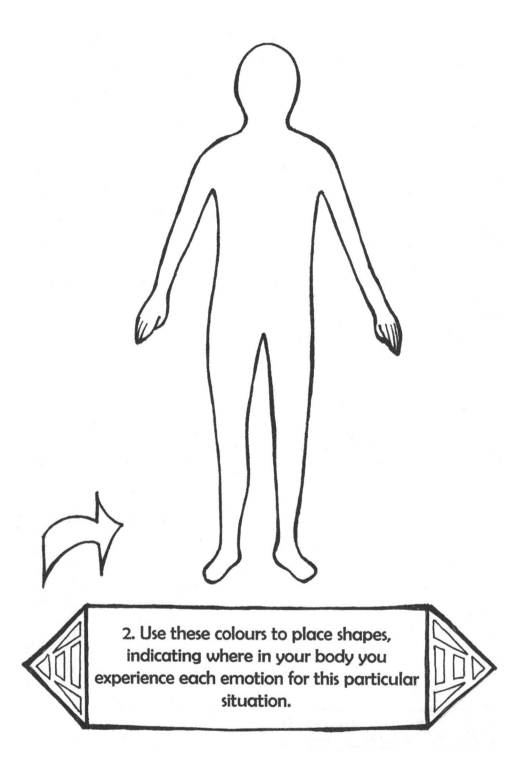

2. Use these colours to place shapes, indicating where in your body you experience each emotion for this particular situation.

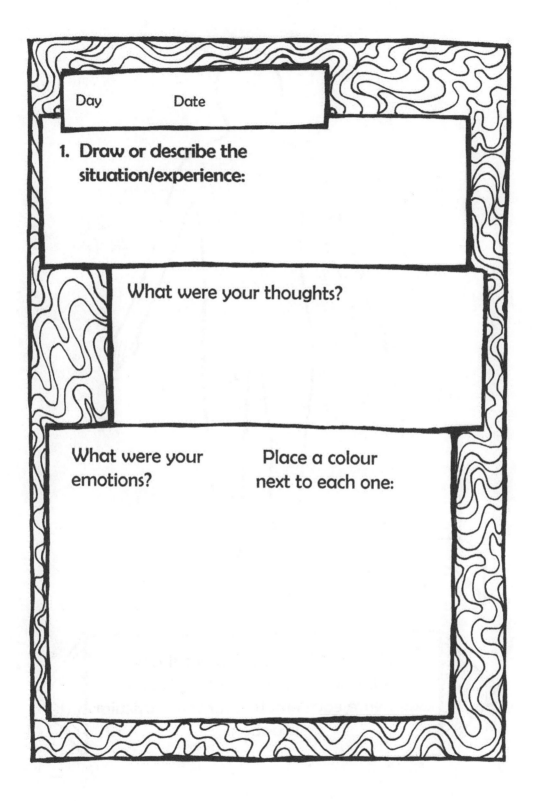

Day   Date

1. Draw or describe the situation/experience:

What were your thoughts?

What were your emotions?   Place a colour next to each one:

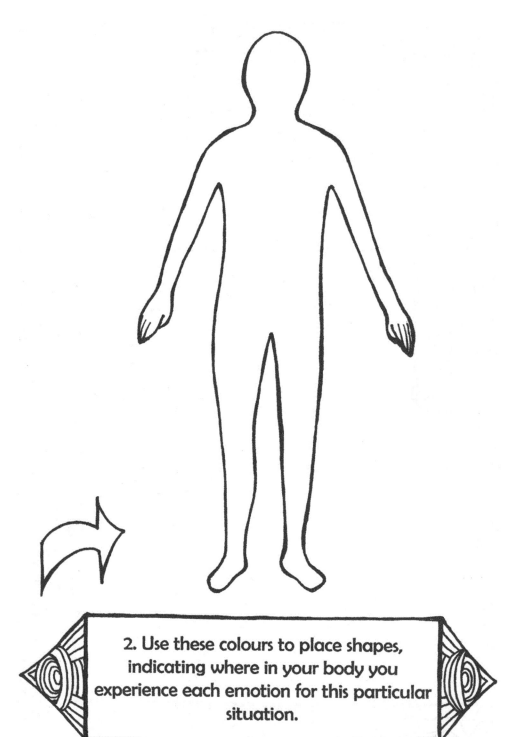

2. Use these colours to place shapes, indicating where in your body you experience each emotion for this particular situation.

4

Motivation

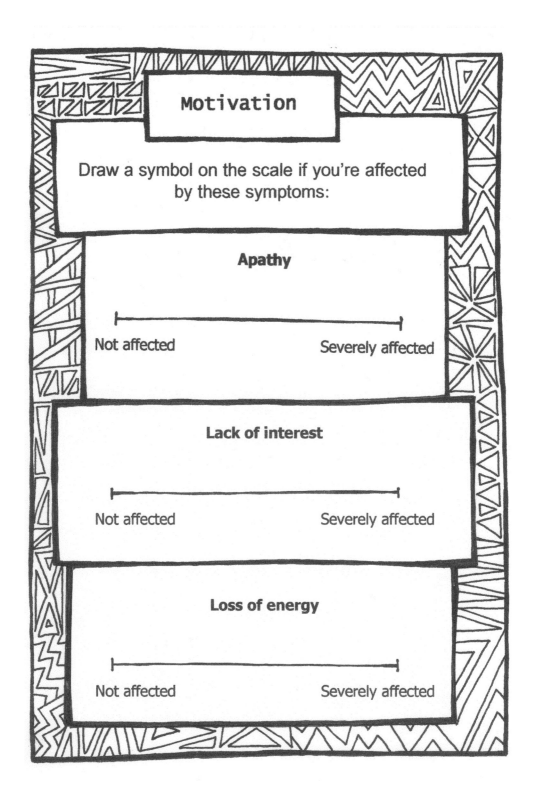

Motivation

Draw a symbol on the scale if you're affected by these symptoms:

Apathy

Not affected ———————————— Severely affected

Lack of interest

Not affected ———————————— Severely affected

Loss of energy

Not affected ———————————— Severely affected

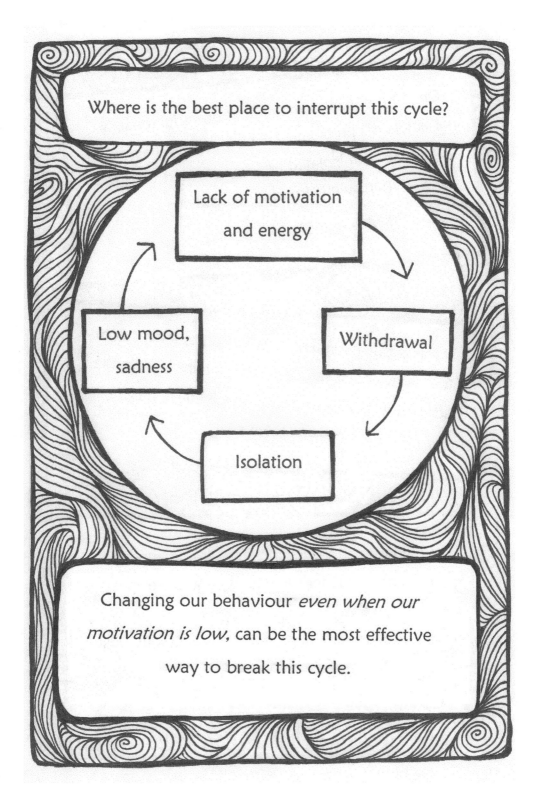

Where is the best place to interrupt this cycle?

Lack of motivation and energy

Withdrawal

Isolation

Low mood, sadness

Changing our behaviour *even when our motivation is low,* can be the most effective way to break this cycle.

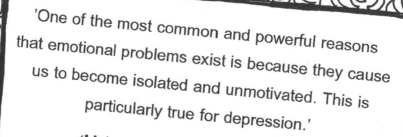

'One of the most common and powerful reasons that emotional problems exist is because they cause us to become isolated and unmotivated. This is particularly true for depression.'

(Myles and Shafran 2015, p.142)

If this is true for you and you're finding it difficult to feel motivated, it can be helpful to think back to the activities you used to enjoy, even if you're no longer doing them now.

The following pages invite you to create images to provide a focus for remembering any previous activities which helped you to feel happy, have a sense of achievement or feel connected with those around you.

Create an image of an activity that used to give you **pleasure**:

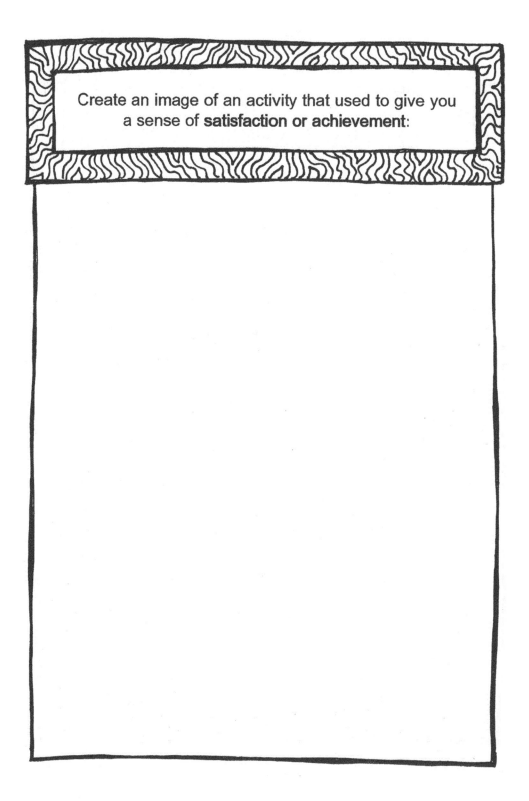

Create an image of an activity that used to give you a sense of **satisfaction or achievement**:

Create an image of an activity that used to give you a sense of **connectedness or closeness** with others:

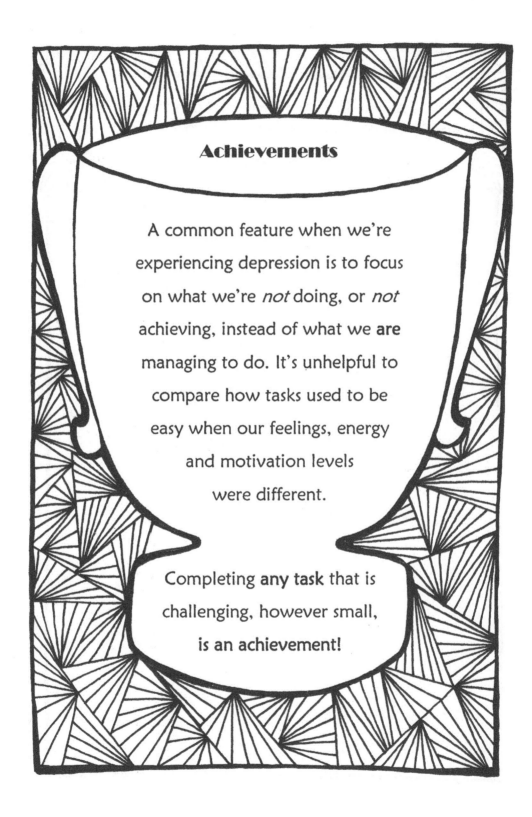

Achievements

A common feature when we're experiencing depression is to focus on what we're *not* doing, or *not* achieving, instead of what we **are** managing to do. It's unhelpful to compare how tasks used to be easy when our feelings, energy and motivation levels were different.

Completing **any task** that is challenging, however small, **is an achievement!**

5

Cognitions

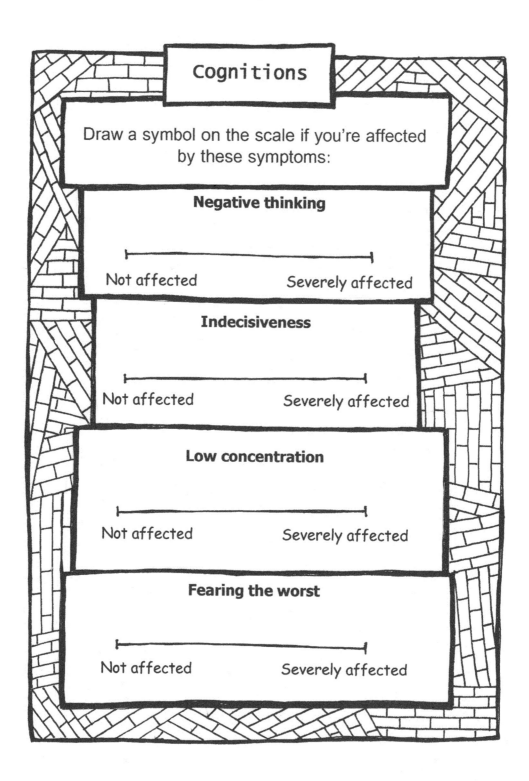

Cognitions

Draw a symbol on the scale if you're affected by these symptoms:

Negative thinking

Not affected   Severely affected

Indecisiveness

Not affected   Severely affected

Low concentration

Not affected   Severely affected

Fearing the worst

Not affected   Severely affected

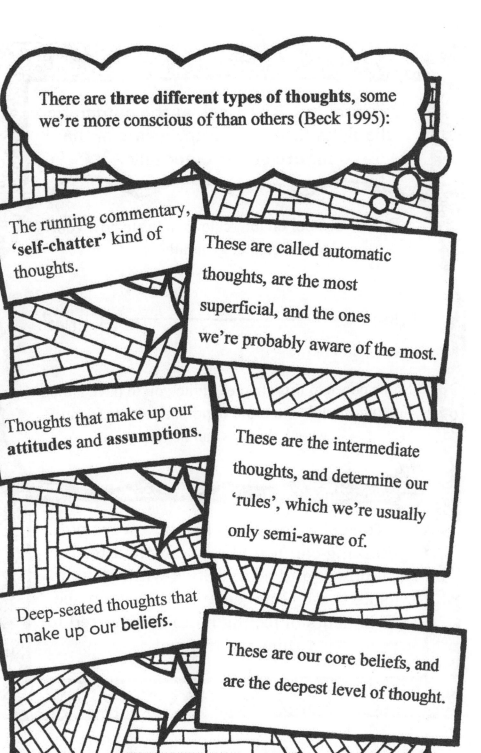

There are **three different types of thoughts**, some we're more conscious of than others (Beck 1995):

The running commentary, **'self-chatter'** kind of thoughts.

These are called automatic thoughts, are the most superficial, and the ones we're probably aware of the most.

Thoughts that make up our **attitudes** and **assumptions**.

These are the intermediate thoughts, and determine our 'rules', which we're usually only semi-aware of.

Deep-seated thoughts that make up our **beliefs**.

These are our core beliefs, and are the deepest level of thought.

It's usual in CBT to look at the automatic thoughts first, to become aware of the nature of our inner talk.

Draw a symbol on the scale to indicate how your self-chatter generally is:

Kind ├─────────────────────────────┤ Critical

Some pages in this chapter invite you to have a look at your thoughts in more depth, in order to identify where changes can be made.

To explore and practise new ways of thinking can feel like a venture into the unknown, and scary. Stick with trying to make these changes and you'll soon see the benefits of feeling more empowered to raise your mood!

The *Compassion Triangle* was developed by Tagar (1995), who identified how we need to have **compassion, love and understanding** for ourselves. This can be expressed initially in our thoughts.

1. We feel low, down or upset

3. We seek out compassion, love and understanding for ourselves

2. We react; we criticise, judge and blame ourselves for feeling this way and our resulting behaviour

How we 'talk' to ourselves, *about* ourselves, is crucial to **how we feel**. If we're constantly being critical or judgemental about everything that we do, think, feel and say, then it will be difficult to feel calm and good about ourselves.

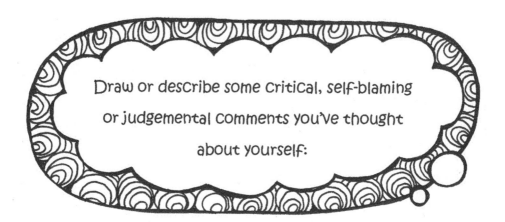

Draw or describe some critical, self-blaming or judgemental comments you've thought about yourself:

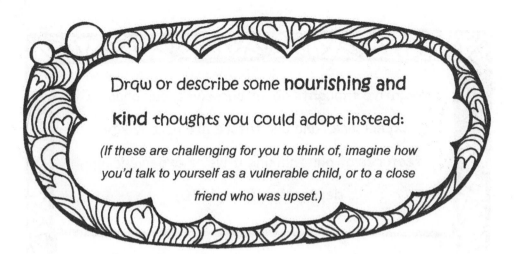

Draw or describe some **nourishing and kind** thoughts you could adopt instead:

(If these are challenging for you to think of, imagine how you'd talk to yourself as a vulnerable child, or to a close friend who was upset.)

Negative thoughts about ourselves, our ongoing experiences and our future are usually key features of our thinking if we're experiencing depression (Beck 1970).

Being unhappy about our life situation can be exacerbated by feeling powerless to change anything, or being unable to imagine how our future could be different. During this time, 'negative thinking tends to centre on the theme of loss or failure to achieve a valued goal.'

(Trower et al. 1991, p.122)

An example could be perceptions of loss or failure due to a relationship break-up, whereby thoughts can be linked to the motivational, affective and behavioural symptoms of depression.

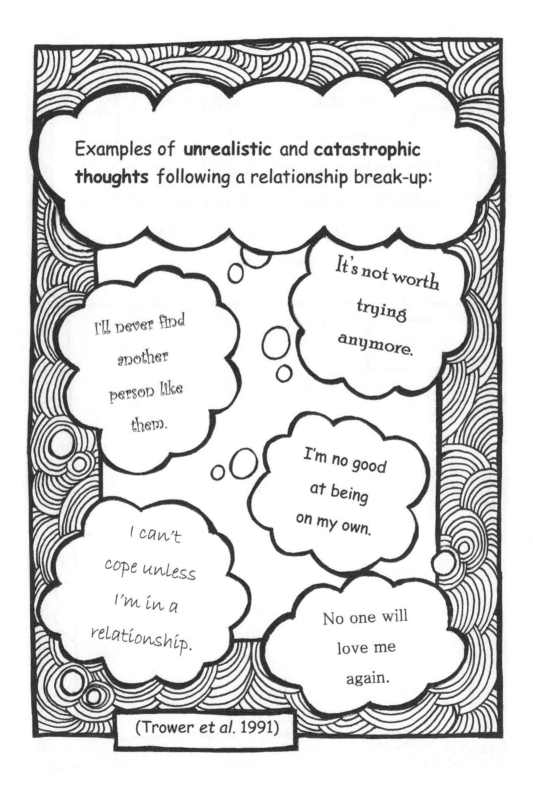

Examples of **unrealistic** and **catastrophic** **thoughts** following a relationship break-up:

It's not worth trying anymore.

I'll never find another person like them.

I'm no good at being on my own.

I can't cope unless I'm in a relationship.

No one will love me again.

(Trower et al. 1991)

Attitudes and assumptions

When certain automatic thoughts become habitual, they can develop into our attitudes and assumptions. Draw or describe any negative views you have about your…

WORK

Boss

Colleagues

Workload

Income

Career

Studies

Draw or describe any negative views you have about your…

FAMILY

Partner

Children

In-laws

Grandparents

Extended family members

Step-family members

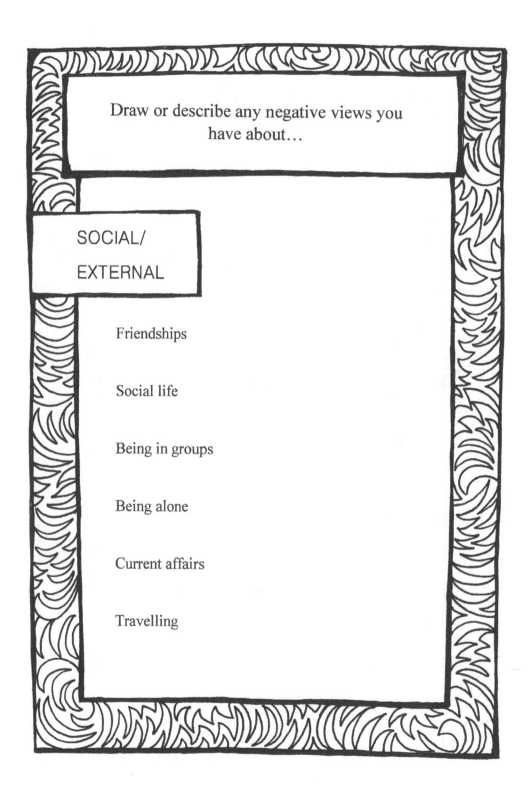

Draw or describe any negative views you have about…

SOCIAL/
EXTERNAL

Friendships

Social life

Being in groups

Being alone

Current affairs

Travelling

Colour in the symbol to show how any negative attitudes and assumptions are going to affect your mood.

Decrease   Stay the same   Increase

We can begin to take control of the thoughts in our mind once we become aware of them and how they're impacting on our emotional state. We can aim to replace these with more positive, realistic or kinder thoughts to develop our attitudes and assumptions.

Return to the previous pages and paint over or cross out any negative thoughts and views.

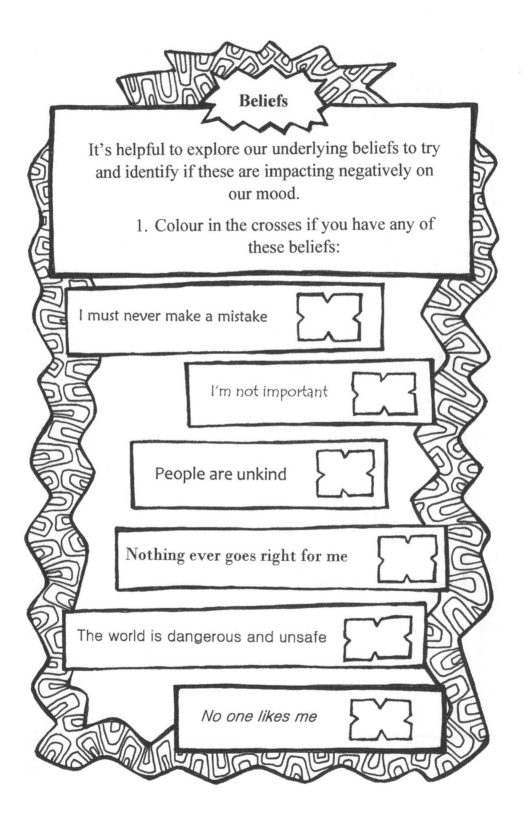

Beliefs

It's helpful to explore our underlying beliefs to try and identify if these are impacting negatively on our mood.

1. Colour in the crosses if you have any of these beliefs:

I must never make a mistake

I'm not important

People are unkind

Nothing ever goes right for me

The world is dangerous and unsafe

No one likes me

2. Draw a symbol on these scales to indicate how realistic you think these beliefs are:

Realistic

Unrealistic

Complete these thought bubbles with some healthier beliefs you could start to develop, which will not make you feel lower. Here are two examples:

It's okay to make mistakes sometimes

Most people are kind

The following pages show some **self-soothing affirmations.**

As soon as you notice your inner self-talk becoming negative or critical, replace these thoughts with an affirmation, such as the ones on the next few pages.

Try repeating them over and over in your mind as you colour in or create images for the phrases. The more often you practise, the easier it will be to remember them and you'll be able to more readily access them in future situations to help prevent symptoms from increasing.

Ideally these will start to develop into your beliefs.

The more familiar you become with positive thoughts and how they feel, the sooner you'll notice when your thoughts are not soothing or nurturing.

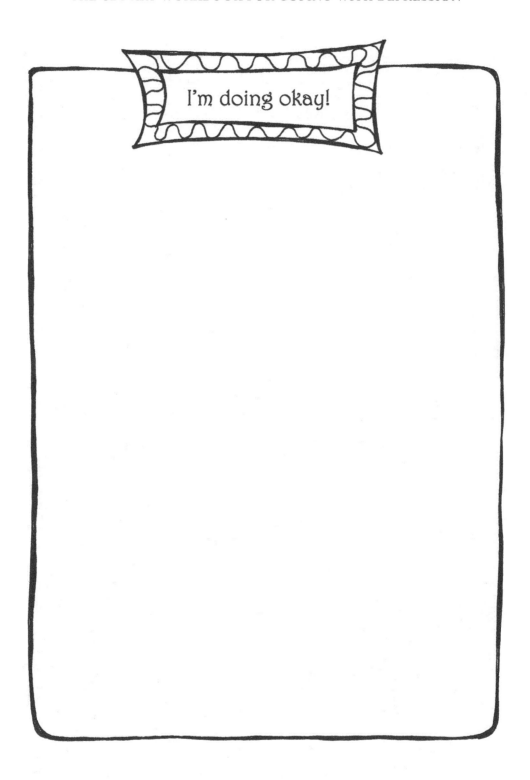

I'm doing okay!

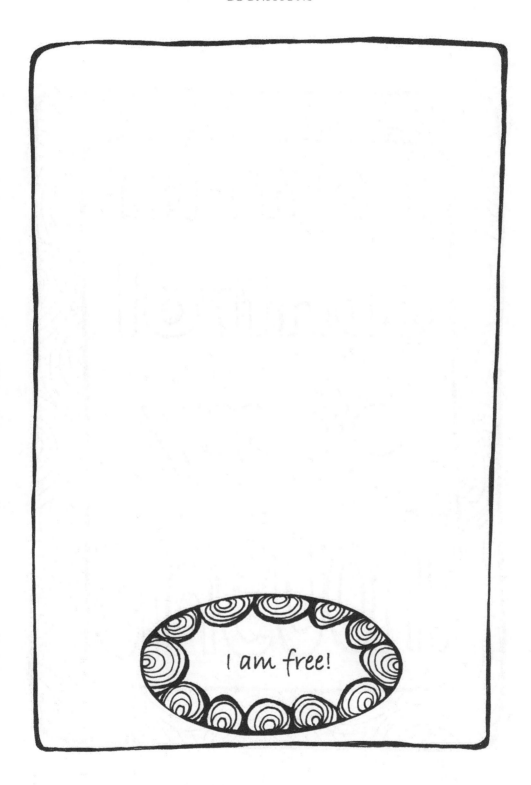

I am free!

I AM IN CONTROL OF MY LIFE

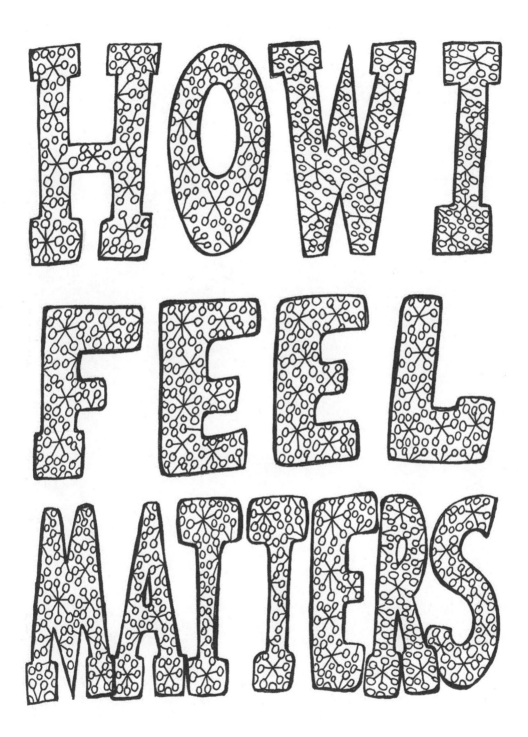

6

Emotions

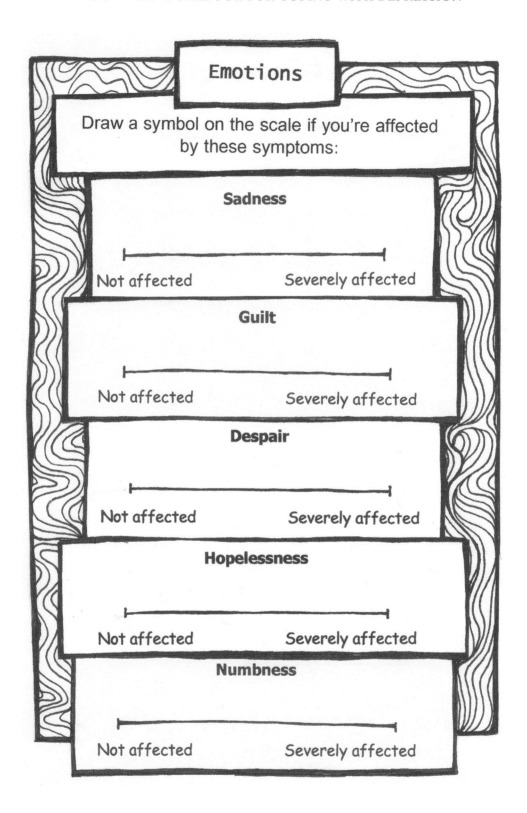

Emotions

Draw a symbol on the scale if you're affected by these symptoms:

Sadness

Not affected   Severely affected

Guilt

Not affected   Severely affected

Despair

Not affected   Severely affected

Hopelessness

Not affected   Severely affected

Numbness

Not affected   Severely affected

Most of us develop strategies (often without realising we're doing it) to deal with difficult emotions which feel uncomfortable, but over time this can cause an increase in intensity in those emotions.

'Sometimes it is difficult or impossible to express feelings with words. Emotions, particularly those that result from trauma, crisis, or loss, are hard to articulate, and often words do not seem to completely convey their meaning. Because feelings are difficult to relate with words, many people push them inward, causing depression, confusion, hopelessness or frustration.

Art making can be particularly beneficial in circumstances where overwhelming or complex emotions need to be expressed. The process of making art may help people confront emotions, overcome depression...and find relief and resolution of grief and loss.'

(Malchiodi 2007, p.133)

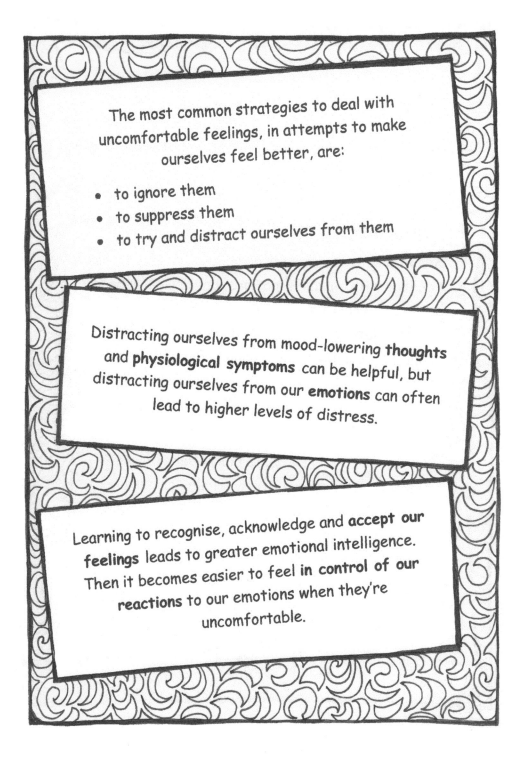

The most common strategies to deal with uncomfortable feelings, in attempts to make ourselves feel better, are:

- to ignore them
- to suppress them
- to try and distract ourselves from them

Distracting ourselves from mood-lowering **thoughts** and **physiological symptoms** can be helpful, but distracting ourselves from our **emotions** can often lead to higher levels of distress.

Learning to recognise, acknowledge and **accept our feelings** leads to greater emotional intelligence. Then it becomes easier to feel **in control of our reactions** to our emotions when they're uncomfortable.

Beliefs about emotions

You can only start to **take control** of your emotions if you **believe that you can,** and this is essential for lowering emotional distress.

(Winch 2018)

Draw a symbol on the scale to show whether you believe your emotions are fixed or malleable:

|————————————————————————|

Fixed   Malleable

'Beliefs that individuals hold about whether emotions are malleable or fixed may play a crucial role in individuals' emotional experiences and their engagement in changing their emotions.'

(Kneeland *et al.* 2016, pp.81–88)

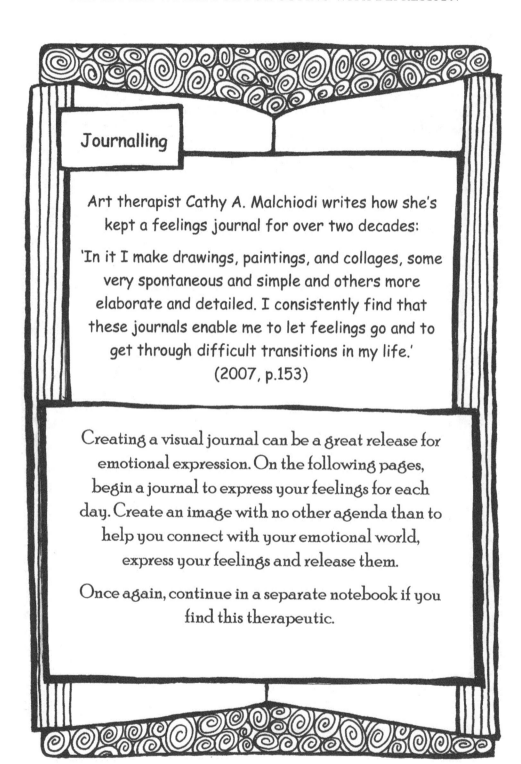

Journalling

Art therapist Cathy A. Malchiodi writes how she's kept a feelings journal for over two decades:

'In it I make drawings, paintings, and collages, some very spontaneous and simple and others more elaborate and detailed. I consistently find that these journals enable me to let feelings go and to get through difficult transitions in my life.'
(2007, p.153)

Creating a visual journal can be a great release for emotional expression. On the following pages, begin a journal to express your feelings for each day. Create an image with no other agenda than to help you connect with your emotional world, express your feelings and release them.

Once again, continue in a separate notebook if you find this therapeutic.

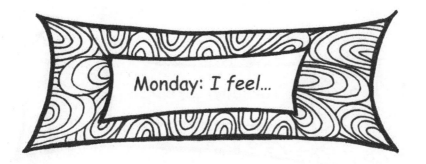

Monday: I feel...

Tuesday: I feel...

Wednesday: *I feel...*

Friday: *I feel...*

7

Behaviour

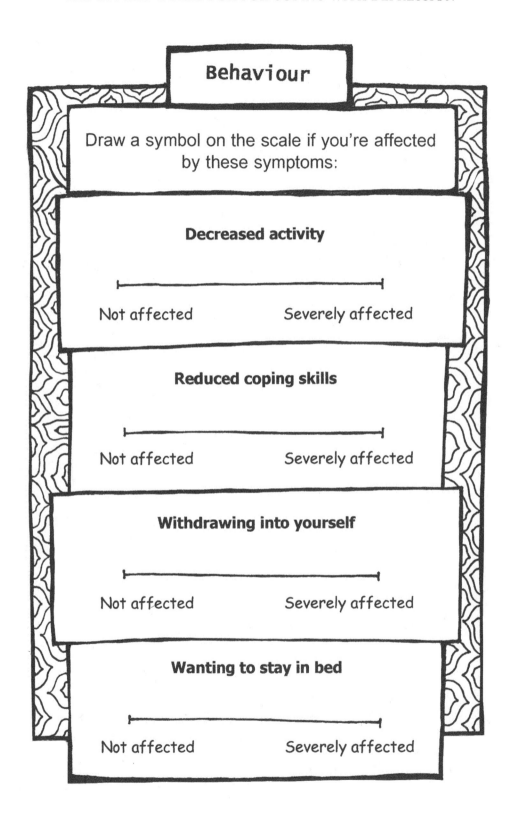

Behaviour

Draw a symbol on the scale if you're affected by these symptoms:

Decreased activity

Not affected   Severely affected

Reduced coping skills

Not affected   Severely affected

Withdrawing into yourself

Not affected   Severely affected

Wanting to stay in bed

Not affected   Severely affected

If we're pro-active about re-establishing a routine by increasing our activities, this can encourage:

- a sense of achievement

- satisfaction

- pleasure

'Research shows that if we change the daily activities that are contributing to the persistence of an emotional problem such as depression, this will often have a positive impact on how we feel. It is no good just finding any old activities to fill up our time. We need to choose activities that are truly important to us and are worthwhile and enjoyable.

It is actually very difficult to feel depressed if you are doing lots of things that are enjoyable or bring a sense of accomplishment.'

(Myles and Shafran 2015, p.148)

ACTIVITY PLANNING

Decreased levels of activity are a common feature of depression. This usually results in us withdrawing from seeing family and friends, and not engaging with activities we previously found enjoyable. Activity planning (Beck *et al.* 1979) focuses on behavioural activation.

'People who experience ongoing feelings of sadness often suffer from a loss of routine. This disruption is likely to worsen an already low mood. Behavioural activation aims to get people active again by helping them to re-establish their normal routines, which in turn improves their mood.'

(Myles and Shafran 2015, p.25)

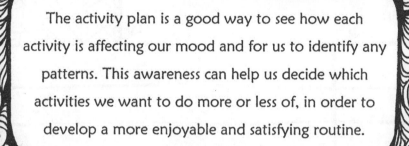

The activity plan is a good way to see how each activity is affecting our mood and for us to identify any patterns. This awareness can help us decide which activities we want to do more or less of, in order to develop a more enjoyable and satisfying routine.

The following pages show plans for a week. If you find this technique helpful and want to use it for longer, you could continue in a separate notebook.

Complete the plans using symbols or words for the time slots. *(Remember to plan some time for completing the following day's table.)*

Then rate each activity for:

- how much you enjoyed it
- your sense of achievement
- how close you felt with others

The last column is for a word or symbol which sums up your mood for each particular activity.

ACTIVITY PLAN for **Monday**

Time

Activity

Enjoyment (0–10)	Achievement (0–10)	Closeness (0–10)	Mood word/ symbol

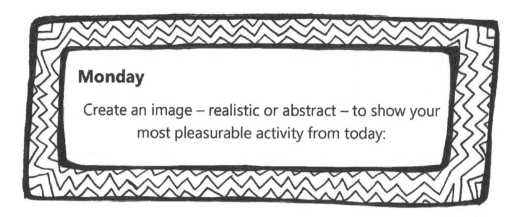

Monday

Create an image – realistic or abstract – to show your most pleasurable activity from today:

Monday

Create an image – realistic or abstract – to show your most satisfying, worthwhile activity from today:

Monday

Create an image – realistic or abstract – to show what your most connected activity from today means to you:

Monday

Create an image – realistic or abstract – to show your
highest level of mood from today:

ACTIVITY PLAN for **Tuesday**

Time

Activity

Enjoyment (0–10)	Achievement (0–10)	Closeness (0–10)	Mood word/ symbol

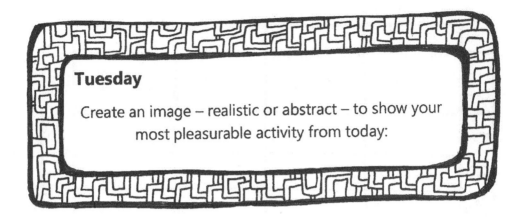

Tuesday

Create an image – realistic or abstract – to show your most pleasurable activity from today:

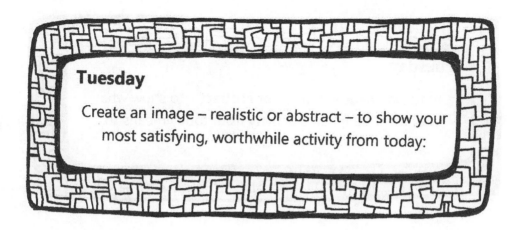

Tuesday

Create an image – realistic or abstract – to show your most satisfying, worthwhile activity from today:

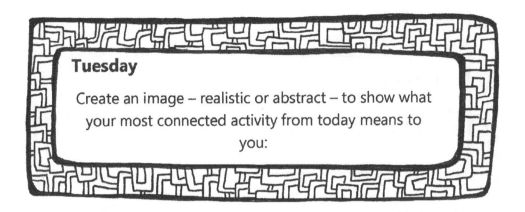

Tuesday

Create an image – realistic or abstract – to show what your most connected activity from today means to you:

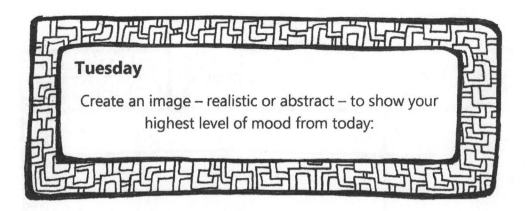

Tuesday

Create an image – realistic or abstract – to show your
highest level of mood from today:

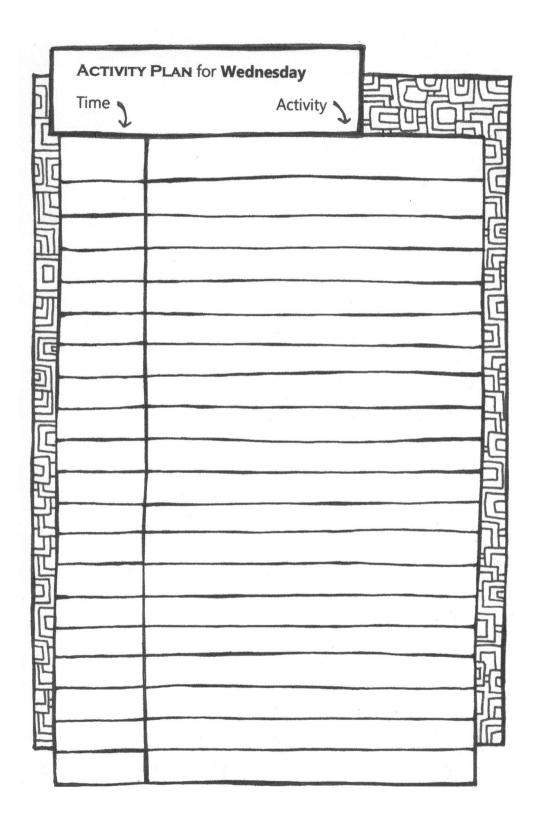

ACTIVITY PLAN for **Wednesday**

Time ↘   Activity ↘

Enjoyment (0–10)	Achievement (0–10)	Closeness (0–10)	Mood word/ symbol

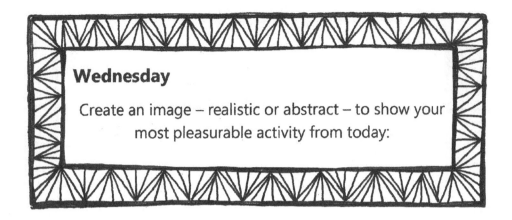

Wednesday

Create an image – realistic or abstract – to show your most pleasurable activity from today:

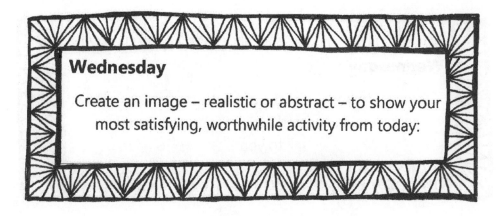

Wednesday

Create an image – realistic or abstract – to show your
most satisfying, worthwhile activity from today:

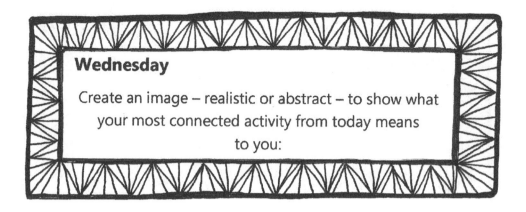

Wednesday

Create an image – realistic or abstract – to show what
your most connected activity from today means
to you:

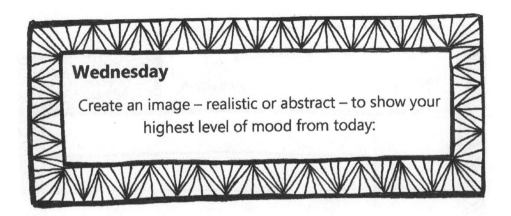

Wednesday

Create an image – realistic or abstract – to show your highest level of mood from today:

ACTIVITY PLAN for Thursday

Time ↓   Activity ↓

Enjoyment (0–10)	Achievement (0–10)	Closeness (0–10)	Mood word/ symbol

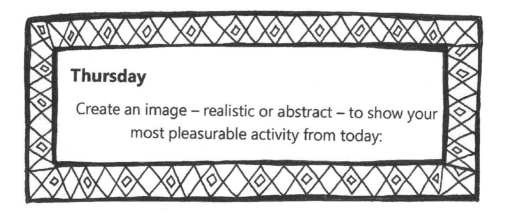

Thursday

Create an image – realistic or abstract – to show your most pleasurable activity from today:

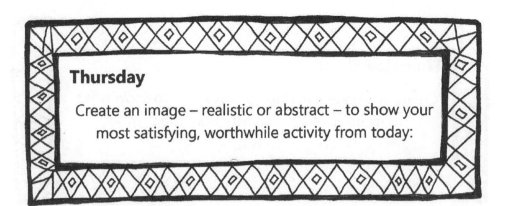

Thursday

Create an image – realistic or abstract – to show your most satisfying, worthwhile activity from today:

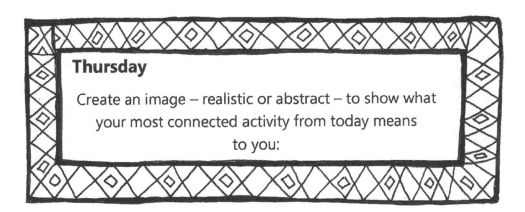

Thursday

Create an image – realistic or abstract – to show what your most connected activity from today means to you:

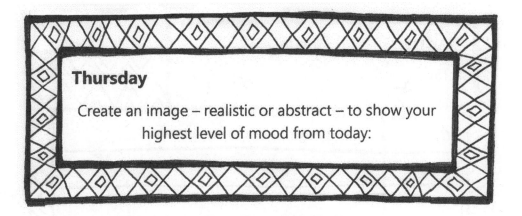

Thursday

Create an image – realistic or abstract – to show your highest level of mood from today:

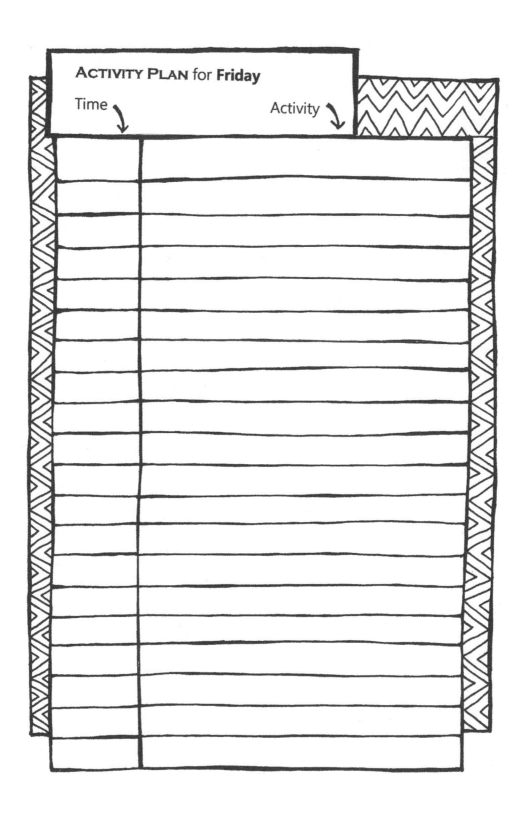

ACTIVITY PLAN for **Friday**

Time

Activity

Enjoyment (0–10)	Achievement (0–10)	Closeness (0–10)	Mood word/ symbol

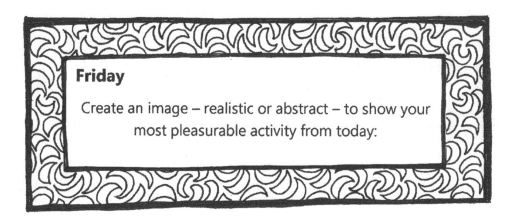

Friday

Create an image – realistic or abstract – to show your most pleasurable activity from today:

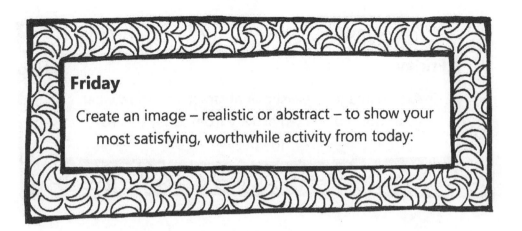

Friday

Create an image – realistic or abstract – to show your most satisfying, worthwhile activity from today:

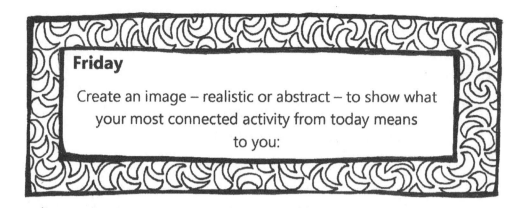

Friday

Create an image – realistic or abstract – to show what your most connected activity from today means to you:

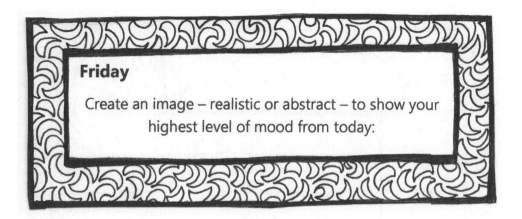

Friday

Create an image – realistic or abstract – to show your highest level of mood from today:

ACTIVITY PLAN for **Saturday**

Time ↓

Activity ↘

Enjoyment (0–10)	Achievement (0–10)	Closeness (0–10)	Mood word/ symbol

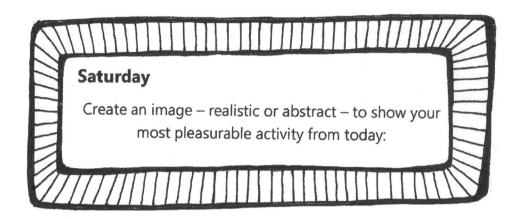

Saturday

Create an image – realistic or abstract – to show your most pleasurable activity from today:

Saturday

Create an image – realistic or abstract – to show your most satisfying, worthwhile activity from today:

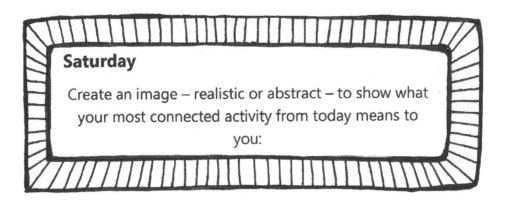

Saturday

Create an image – realistic or abstract – to show what your most connected activity from today means to you:

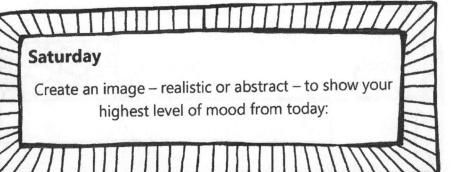

Saturday

Create an image – realistic or abstract – to show your highest level of mood from today:

ACTIVITY PLAN for **Sunday**

Time ↓   Activity ↘

Enjoyment (0–10)	Achievement (0–10)	Closeness (0–10)	Mood word/ symbol

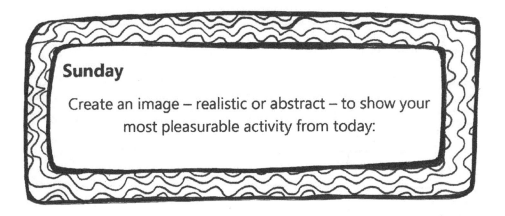

Sunday

Create an image – realistic or abstract – to show your most pleasurable activity from today:

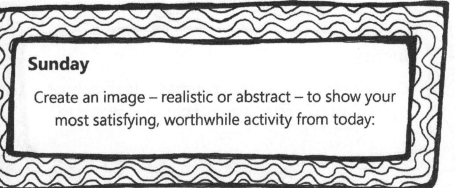

Sunday

Create an image – realistic or abstract – to show your most satisfying, worthwhile activity from today:

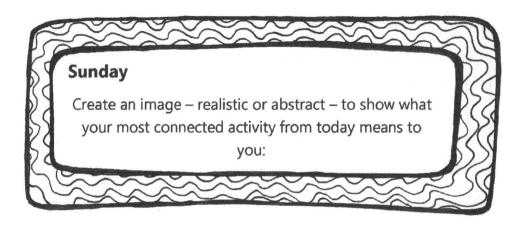

Sunday

Create an image – realistic or abstract – to show what your most connected activity from today means to you:

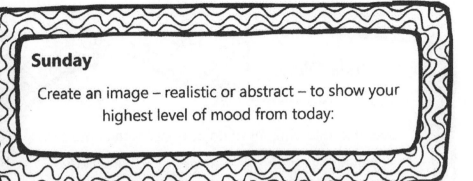

Sunday

Create an image – realistic or abstract – to show your
highest level of mood from today:

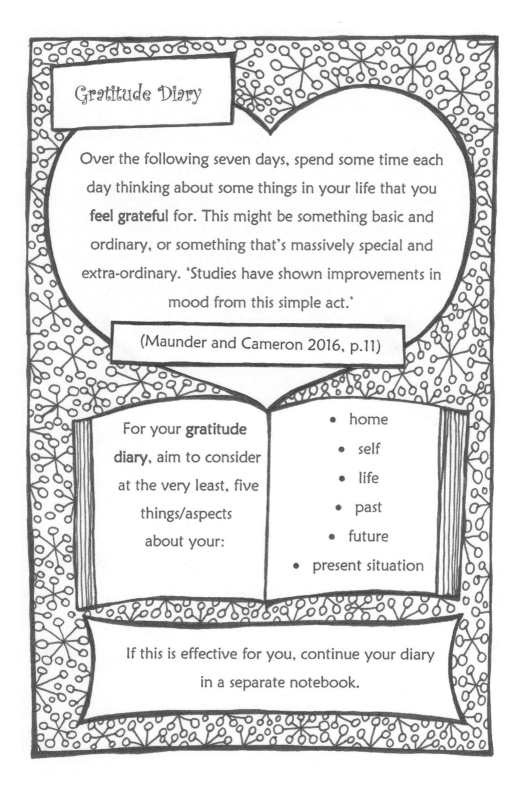

Gratitude Diary

Over the following seven days, spend some time each day thinking about some things in your life that you **feel grateful** for. This might be something basic and ordinary, or something that's massively special and extra-ordinary. 'Studies have shown improvements in mood from this simple act.'

(Maunder and Cameron 2016, p.11)

For your **gratitude diary**, aim to consider at the very least, five things/aspects about your:

- home
- self
- life
- past
- future
- present situation

If this is effective for you, continue your diary in a separate notebook.

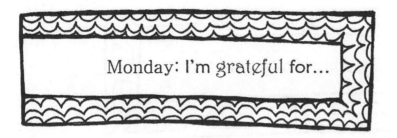

Monday: I'm grateful for...

Wednesday: I'm grateful for...

Thursday: I'm grateful for...

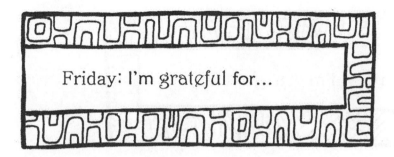

Friday: I'm grateful for...

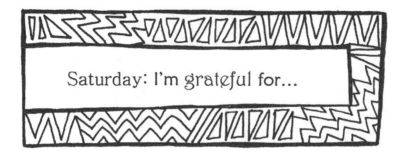

Saturday: I'm grateful for...

Sunday: I'm grateful for...

8

Physiology

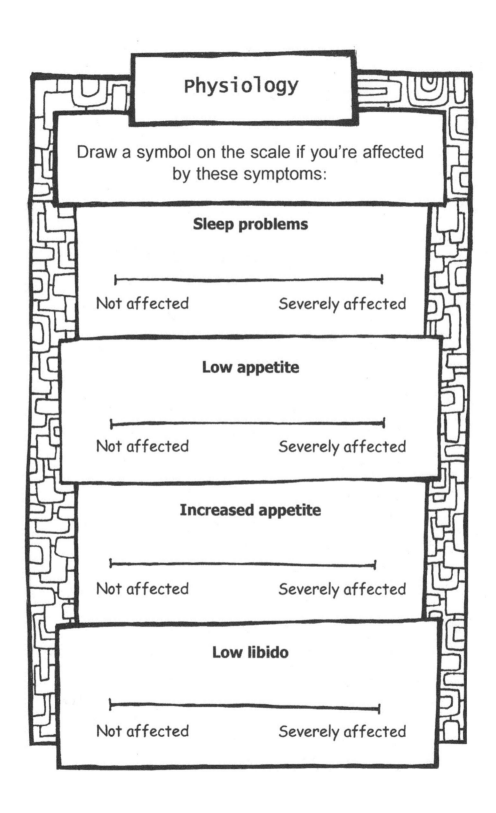

Physiology

Draw a symbol on the scale if you're affected by these symptoms:

Sleep problems

Not affected ————————————————— Severely affected

Low appetite

Not affected ————————————————— Severely affected

Increased appetite

Not affected ————————————————— Severely affected

Low libido

Not affected ————————————————— Severely affected

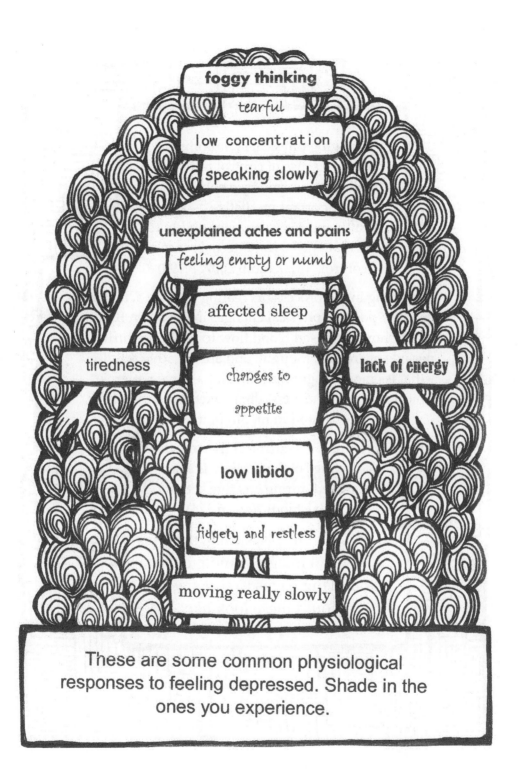

foggy thinking

tearful

low concentration

speaking slowly

unexplained aches and pains

feeling empty or numb

affected sleep

tiredness

lack of energy

changes to appetite

low libido

fidgety and restless

moving really slowly

These are some common physiological responses to feeling depressed. Shade in the ones you experience.

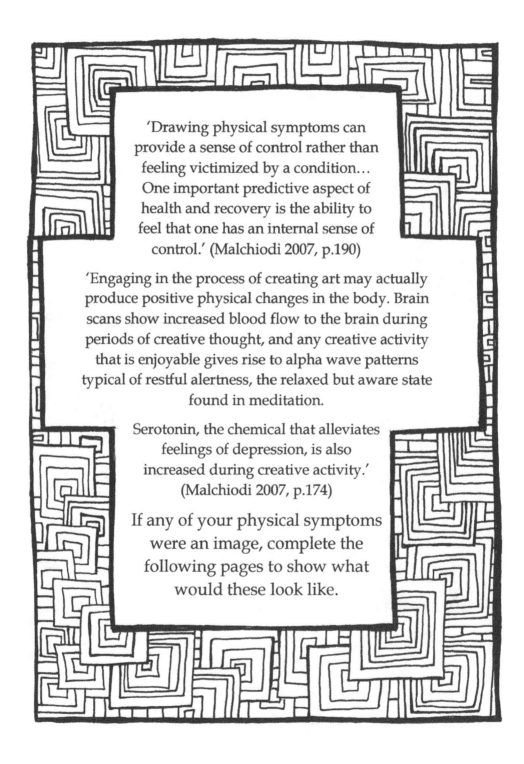

'Drawing physical symptoms can provide a sense of control rather than feeling victimized by a condition… One important predictive aspect of health and recovery is the ability to feel that one has an internal sense of control.' (Malchiodi 2007, p.190)

'Engaging in the process of creating art may actually produce positive physical changes in the body. Brain scans show increased blood flow to the brain during periods of creative thought, and any creative activity that is enjoyable gives rise to alpha wave patterns typical of restful alertness, the relaxed but aware state found in meditation.

Serotonin, the chemical that alleviates feelings of depression, is also increased during creative activity.' (Malchiodi 2007, p.174)

If any of your physical symptoms were an image, complete the following pages to show what would these look like.

1. Physical symptom

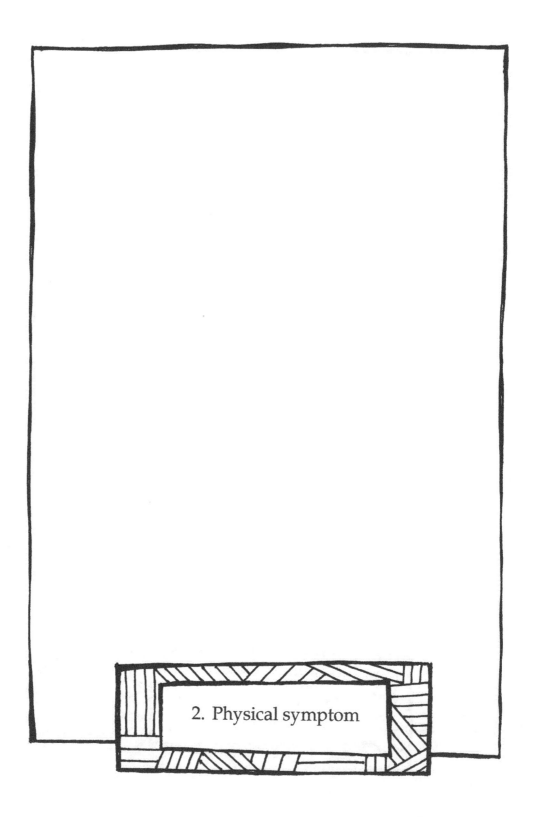

2. Physical symptom

3. Physical symptom

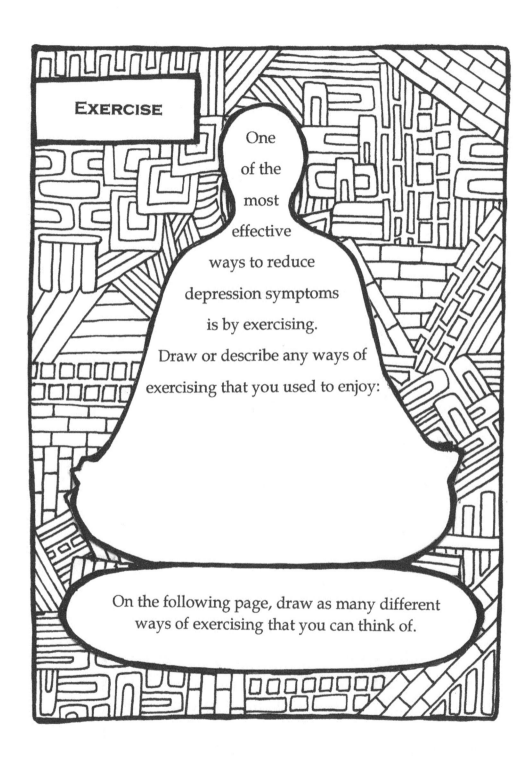

EXERCISE

One of the most effective ways to reduce depression symptoms is by exercising. Draw or describe any ways of exercising that you used to enjoy:

On the following page, draw as many different ways of exercising that you can think of.

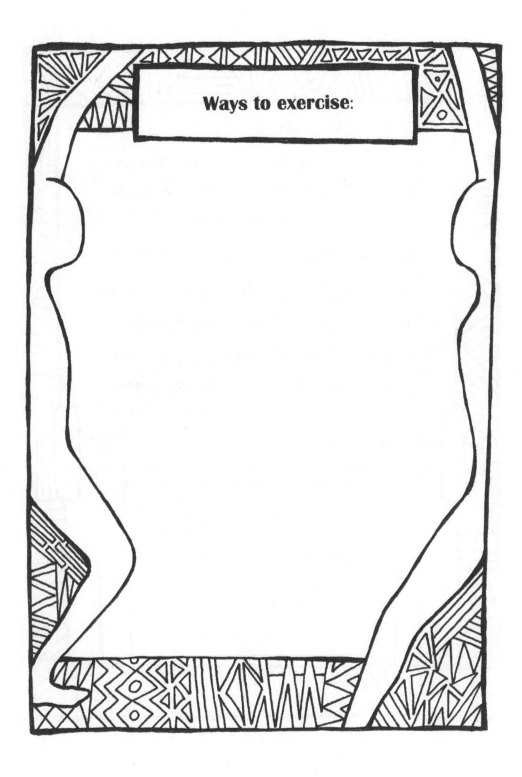

Ways to exercise:

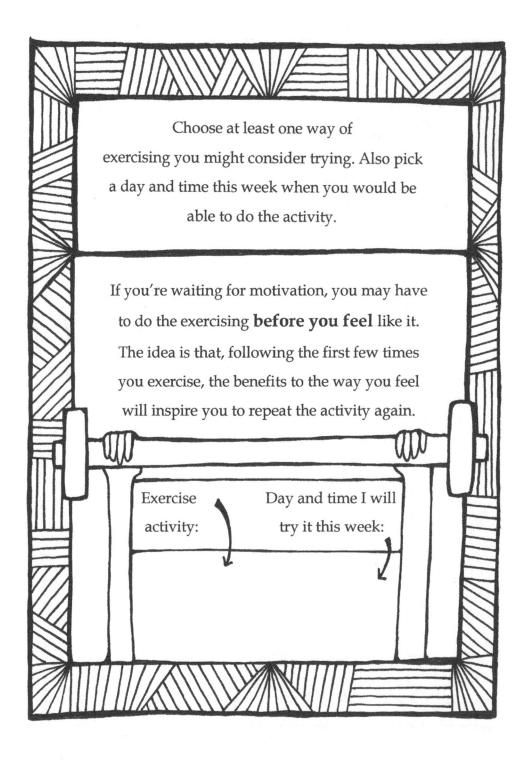

Choose at least one way of exercising you might consider trying. Also pick a day and time this week when you would be able to do the activity.

If you're waiting for motivation, you may have to do the exercising **before you feel** like it. The idea is that, following the first few times you exercise, the benefits to the way you feel will inspire you to repeat the activity again.

Exercise activity:

Day and time I will try it this week:

9

Resilience

RESILIENCE

This is the ability to bounce back from life's challenges. We can learn to develop resilience! This can be done by focusing time and effort on ourselves: physically, mentally and emotionally. Spending time doing things like this workbook is a good example.

If you had to do **one kind thing** for yourself at least **once a day,** what kinds of ideas would you appreciate as a treat for yourself? On the following page, draw or describe as many ideas as you can think of to go in your resilience toolkit.

Examples could be:

- Being in nature
- Taking a leisurely bath
- Watching a funny or uplifting film
- Reading an inspiring novel

My **resilience** toolkit

Wellbeing box

You could create an actual box of things you find comforting. Inside it could be anything that's important and personal to you, such as photos of loved ones, memorabilia from happy experiences, images you find soothing to look at, a pebble you like the shape of...

A 'positives' notebook could be added to your box, where you record any compliments you receive, any positive comments from others about you, and things which make you feel good inside.

When you're feeling low you can access your box and spend a few moments focusing on your chosen things, to help raise your mood.

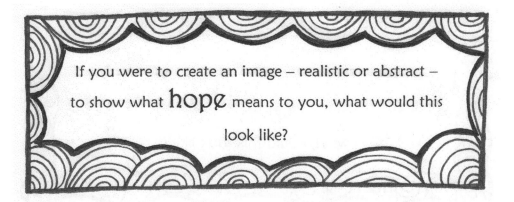

If you were to create an image – realistic or abstract – to show what **hope** means to you, what would this look like?

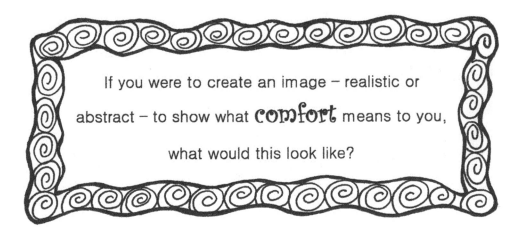

If you were to create an image – realistic or abstract – to show what **comfort** means to you, what would this look like?

If you were to create an image – realistic or abstract – to show what contentment means to you, what would this look like?

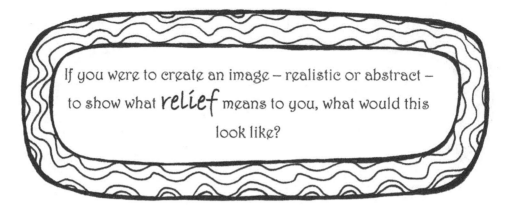

If you were to create an image – realistic or abstract – to show what **relief** means to you, what would this look like?

10

In Control

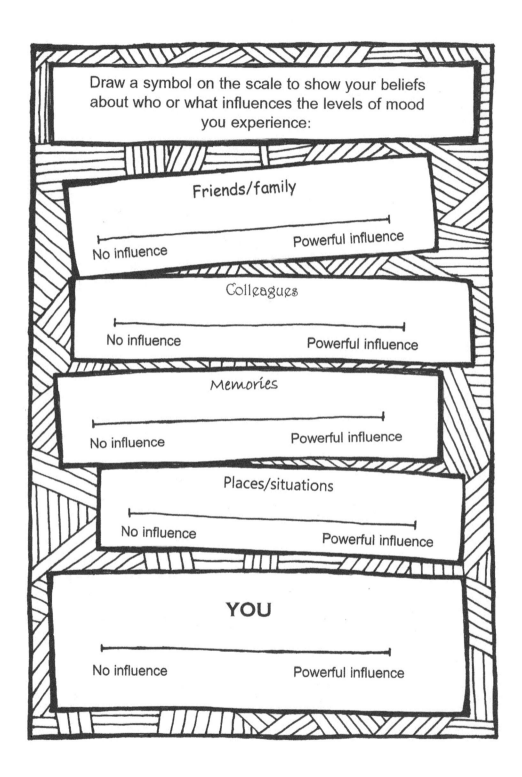

Draw a symbol on the scale to show your beliefs about who or what influences the levels of mood you experience:

Friends/family

No influence — Powerful influence

Colleagues

No influence — Powerful influence

Memories

No influence — Powerful influence

Places/situations

No influence — Powerful influence

YOU

No influence — Powerful influence

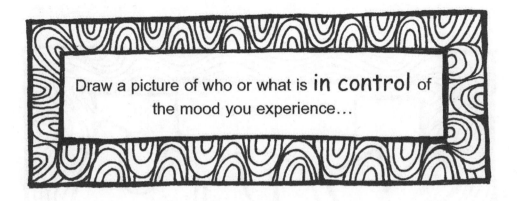

Draw a picture of who or what is **in control** of the mood you experience…

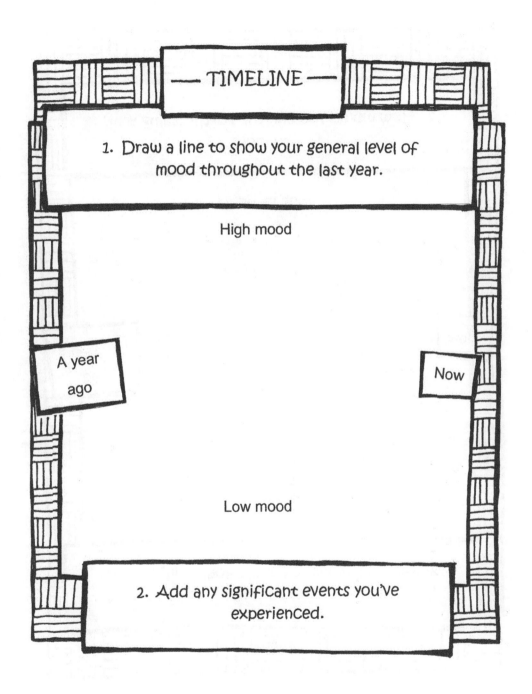

— TIMELINE —

1. Draw a line to show your general level of mood throughout the last year.

High mood

A year ago

Now

Low mood

2. Add any significant events you've experienced.

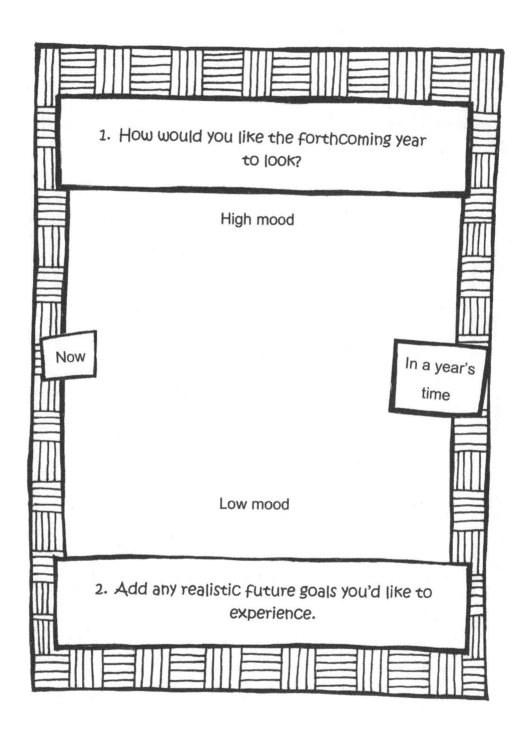

1. How would you like the forthcoming year to look?

High mood

Now

In a year's time

Low mood

2. Add any realistic future goals you'd like to experience.

Congratulations!

By making efforts such as completing this workbook and putting in time to focus on changing and raising your levels of mood, this demonstrates how much you're willing to take more control of...

- your life
- your wellbeing
- your mental health
- your future
- the person you want to be

...and in turn, this takes courage and strength. I hope you can acknowledge this for the achievement that it already is!

References

Barford, D. (2018) 'Dark night of the soul.' *Therapy Today*, Vol. 29:6.

Beck, A.T. (1970) 'The Core Problems in Depression: The Cognitive Triad.' In J. Masserman (ed.) *Depression: Theories and Therapies*. New York, NY: Grune & Straton.

Beck, J.S. (1995) *Cognitive Therapy: Basics and Beyond*. New York, NY: Guildford Press.

Beck, J.S., Rush A.J., Shaw, B.F. and Emery, G. (1979) *Cognitive Therapy of Depression*. New York, NY: Guildford Press.

Dunn, K. (2016) *Understanding Depression*. Available at: www.mind.org.uk/media/4616615/understanding-depression-2016.pdf.

Jenkins, P. (2017) *Professional Practice in Counselling & Psychotherapy*. London: Sage.

Kneeland, E.T., Dovidio, J.F., Joormann, J. and Clark, M.S. (2016) 'Emotion malleability beliefs.' *Clinical Psychology Review*, April 45:81–88. Available at: www.ncbi.nlm.nih.gov/pubmed/27086086.

Layard, R. (2006) *The Depression Report: A New Deal for Depression and Anxiety Disorders*. Centre for Economic Performance Mental Health Policy Group. Available at: eprints.lse.ac.uk/818/1/DEPRESSION_REPORT_LAYARD.pdf.

London, P. (1989) *No More Secondhand Art: Awakening the Artist Within*. Boston, MA: Shambala.

Malchiodi, C.A. (2007) *The Art Therapy Sourcebook*. New York, NY: McGraw Hill.

Maunder, L. and Cameron, L. (2016) *Depression and Low Mood*. Newcastle: Northumberland, Tyne and Wear NHS Foundation Trust.

Myles, P. and Shafran, R. (2015) *The CBT Handbook*. London: Robinson.

Neenan, M. and Dryden, W. (2004) *Cognitive Therapy: 100 Key Points & Techniques*. Hove: Brunner Routledge.

Tagar, Y. (1995) 'Compassion: A path of self-healing.' *Golden Age Magazine*, Jul/Aug, 25–28.

Trower, P., Casey, A. and Dryden, W. (1991) *Cognitive Behavioural Counselling in Action*. London: Sage.

Winch, G. (2018) 'Why You Should Believe You Can Control Your Emotions.' *Psychology Today* (posted 5 Sep 18). Available at: www.psychologytoday.com/gb/blog/the-squeaky-wheel/201809/why-you-should-believe-you-can-control-your-emotions.